Part biography, part succinct histor the viewpoint of an innocent 21-yea Women's Royal Air Force (WRAF) and was sent out to Berlin in 1948. She now looks back at that time and how her views have been changed in the intervening years.

Admittedly, thinking that she was a dog and that a suitable canine accommodation had been supplied rather than the usual billet is just one of the interesting anecdotal stories within the book. It can be read as her personal journey or as an interesting historical document that looks at many of the wider political and social issues in the lead up to the Berlin Airlift.

The Bridge of Wings

Joyce Hargrave-Wright

Abilitywise LLP
2015

Copyright © 2015 by:

Joyce.Hargrave-Wright

The right of Joyce Hargrave-Wright to be identified as author of this Work has been asserted by her in accordance with sections 77 and 78 of the Copyright, Designs and Patents Act 1988.

All rights reserved. No part of this publication may be reproduced, stored in retrieval system, copied in any form or by any means, electronic, mechanical, photocopying, recording or otherwise transmitted without written permission from the publisher.

ISBN 978-0-9928588-5-8

Published by Abilitywise LLP
Reg Office: Homeside Cottage,
Barrington Road,
Torquay
TQ1 2QJ

Email: info@abilitywise.co.uk

www.abilitywise.com

Abilitywise LLP is a partnership that works with people who have disabilities. Its publication emphasis is aimed at information relevant to its client group or to producing fiction and other material written or created by those who are deemed to have a disability.

Dedication

This book is dedicated to Miles Heasman, a fellow member of my History Group, who encouraged me to look for the links between peoples and countries.

Contents

Acknowledgements.......................................(ix)
Chapter 1 - Background...................................1
Chapter 2 - The Start of My Journey...................27
Chapter 3 - Life at the Camp...........................47
Chapter 4 - And Afterwards.............................73
Bibliography 99
Appendix 1- Diary of Events – 1948 to 1949........101
Appendix 2 - Aircraft Facts and Figures.............108
Appendix 3 - Names of those who lost their lives...110

ACKNOWLEDGEMENTS

There were many friends and colleagues who helped to recall my involvement during those far-off days serving on the Berlin Airlift. Apologies to those I have neglected to mention. Put it done to an overcrowded memory!

I thank Sue Campbell with her constant fund of information, Bill and Flo Ball, Juergen Balke, Bernard Maeder, Gunther Herzog, Frau Baerbel E. Simon, Geoff Lipscombe and members of the Bad Eilsen Reunion, Jean Eastham, Gordon and Gloria Westwell and members of the British Berlin Airlift Association, Ann Lewis-Jones, my history course leader, with her depth of knowledge and insight.

My sister Audrey remembers my going off into the unknown depths of Europe and was one of the few who managed to get letters to me and especially on my 21st birthday. All my family members have been supportive and have cheered me on my way. My sincere thanks to Julian, who guided me through the maze of the lay-out, copyright, the pictures and contributed so much in the way of illustrating and the publishing and my less than adequate technology skills.

Chapter 1- Background

What was I doing at the bottom of a 90 foot deep stairway into the bowels of the earth?

Being claustrophobic, this was not the best place for me to be working, especially as my official focus was firmly on the skies above.

I had joined the WRAF (Women's Royal Air Force) after the 1939-45 war, partly because of peer persuasion and some nebulous feelings of country loyalty. This action also seemed a good chance to establish my own identity as from leaving school and taking some temporary employment, I had the need of a 20 year old, to search for a future that would satisfy my ambitions, rather more than the aspirations of my education mentors and my parents, who had always envisaged an academic future for their children.

Having worked in a school, and education still attracting a certain cache in those far off days, I was elevated to Clerk Special Duties, after my initial training. I was sent to Bawdsey, in Suffolk and examined the intricacies of the RADAR screen. Later, I trained at Stanmore and at Uxbridge in certain aspects of Air Traffic Control and it was at Uxbridge that I crept my way down the 90 steps each duty, wondering whether I would get there without collapse and even more importantly, whether I would ever get out again.

I was a 'hoe' girl, using the magnetic rod that hovered over a table map, plotting the movements and speed of aircraft. The rod was thus named because of the similarity of its shape to the garden implement! This was hard work, mainly because of the concentration required to maintain the exact whereabouts of the aircraft, which during the war, would have been enemy aircraft, as well as our own craft. The importance of the work therefore, was immense during the war years. For me and my fellow 'erks' (new recruits and lowest of ranks), we carried on the tradition of the work ethic that had, for me, begun with RADAR training. In reality, in 1947, we plotted non-existent 'planes most of the time.

I suppose it never ever occurred to me that one day, I would be grateful for all my training and the patience of the trainers. I was as surprised as anyone, particularly my parents, who thought that travelling 'abroad' was akin to a descent into Sodom and Gomorrah, when I was sent to Germany, to take part in a venture that was to keep the Berliners alive for a whole year. Looking back, I can appreciate the depth of my then ignorance of the reasons as to why the airlifting of food and coal and myriad commodities was necessary. In the last few years, I have researched quite extensively and read many books ostensibly giving accurate representations of the Blockade and the political and humane reasons for its inception. I have been surprised, shocked, amused sometimes and even angry, to find that rarely have books, articles, lectures or reports, agreed on supposed facts.

One glaring instance, is the date that the first load was delivered to Berlin, which changes according to the source of my information. It seems to me that literature generally is coloured by the subjective view of the writer and this is certainly the case with the reporting of the Berlin Airlift. There are books that only consider the American input and the British and other nations are hardly mentioned. Fewer books are written by British authors on the Blockade and over the years, we do seem to have lost our true identity, with the regard to the importance of our involvement. In fact, we often effected tasks that were not touched by others. For example, we carried all the 'wet' loads, some of which were dangerous, such as oil. It could be said too, that we had the monopoly of the civilian transportation, in and out of Berlin and of Germany itself.

In retrospect, I now consider that 1948, the year of the Berlin Airlift was pivotal in my life and coloured my whole concept of the politics of Europe, which are sadly, still in turmoil, in 2015. I am therefore writing this book, not only to record my very small involvement in the Berlin airlift, but to see if I now understand more clearly why it was so necessary then, to protect all those in West Berlin and then attempt to piece together the current state of Europe. I have included examples of material that have been presented to me after 1948 and indeed are still becoming available to me so, that I am constantly discovering that circumstances, events, places, even the work that I did on a day to day basis, can look very different from afar.

Records, books, the recollections of the Airlift by others, newly published research, the exhibitions of artifacts and the re-thinking of my own memories, have sometimes proved me to have been mistaken in the conclusions and judgements that I made at the time. It has been an enlightening and interesting time for me.

To feed a city from the air,
Impossible they were aware.
So many aircraft they would need,
Two million souls that they must feed.
Among them all, there were a few,
We have a plan, this we can do.
And those with faith, they did supply,
A Bridge of Wings through Berlin Sky.

(From song, 'A Bridge of Wings', written and composed by Wm.(Bill) Ball, Served on Berlin Airlift at Wunstorf, Fassburg and Lubeck. Flight Line, 77 Squadron)

Bill Ball 2006

It would be pertinent at this point to set a very brief background scene to the political situation in which I found myself, when I was sent as a uniformed but uninformed airwoman, to Germany in June 1948. I can only write with any personal authority about the events, incidents and my perceptions, as I experienced them at the time. Even then, since that period in my life, the world has changed, technology has caught up with us and in my case, has often left me behind. However, through my own ignorance at the time, information that was not known or understood by me in 1948 about the Airlift, Germany and indeed the world, has now come to my attention, mainly through personal research, plus the easier access to knowledge gained from various media.

With maturity, I have grown in my understanding of the reasons for the need for the Airlift and the ramifications that could have resulted had it failed. I have had many 'Damascus' episodes, when I have realised that I was mistaken in some of the conclusions that I made all those years ago. I have also become fascinated by the historical background to the Airlift and so now appreciate more the consequences that have occurred since that eventful time in my life.

A member of the history course that I have attended over the past few years, has always been interested in the 'links' between the countries of the world and how peoples living in one spot can change regimes and even their nationalities, many times. Borders have constantly altered and the lands and territories themselves have changed hands, ownership and control. Even during my lifetime, countries have amalgamated and then divided again, two prime examples being in Yugoslavia and Russia. The German/Russian relationship has ranged from co-operation, to a full war situation. Lands have been sequestered and then re-gained, sometimes manoeuvred by means of royal marriages between nations.

Nevertheless the chief aims, have been those of 'control', often with the ultimate goal of world domination. I think of Ghengis Khan galloping across half of the earth's surface taking mastery of more and more lands and expanding his domains. Reasons and circumstances for this pursuit of power may differ and control has often been sought for political and religious convictions, but finally the ownership of the land and therefore the domination of the peoples, still remain the priority. Wars then become inevitable and the history of our world has become a roller coaster of extremes and changes.

Wikipedia *(Google Encyclopaedia, Germany/Russia Relations 23.4.2014),* suggested that we know little about the earliest connection between the Germans and the Slavs and that any meaningful contact can be traced to the campaigns of the Teutonic Knights in the Baltic regions, where they took control of the land. In fact before the 18th century, Russia had little interest in German affairs, made difficult by the fact that Germany was composed of many small states, although under the nominal headship of the Holy Roman Emperor

Germans gradually migrated eastwards, mainly into the Slavonic areas, particularly those that were adjacent to Russian controlled territories. German farmers, all kinds of traders and businessmen moved into many lands, including Prussia, the Baltic countries, Poland, Slovenia and the Ukrainian area. So successful were they, that often their expertise was welcomed by the Russian Government, allowing the Germans to become the dominant land owners and the leaders of the business enterprises. The kingdom of Prussia was created in 1701 and with the public declaration of the Russian Empire, in 1721, the two states started to interact with each other. However, as I suggested at the outset, change was constant and countries changed positions and allegiances, as often as the Vicar of Bray, the subject of an anonymous poet, in 1734 or thereabouts, who wrote satirically about a vicar who lived during the reigns of Henry 8th, Edward 6th and his sisters, Queen Mary and Queen Elizabeth 1st, with the dominant religion changing from Papist to Protestant, thence to Papist, then Protestant again. The Vicar remained loyal to them all, mainly to save his own head.

The Vicar of Bray
Anonymous satire from The British Musical Miscellany 1734

In Good King Charles's golden days,
When Loyalty no harm meant,
A Furious High-Church Man I was,
And so I gain'd Preferment
Unto my Flock, I daily Preach'd,
Kings are by God Appointed,

Ana Damn'd are those who dare resist,
Or touch the Lord's Annointed.

And this is Law, I will maintain
Until my Dying Day, Sir,
That whatsoever King shall reign,
I will be Vicar of Bray, Sir.

When Royal James, possest the Crown,
And Popery grew in fashion,
The Penal Law I houted down,
And read the Declaration:
The Church of Rome, I found would fit,
Full well, my Constitution,
And I had been a Jesuit,
But for the revolution. (And This is Law etc.)

When William, our Deliverer came,
To heal the Nations Grievance,
I turn'd the Cat in Pan again,
And swore to him Allegiance,
Old Principles I did revoke,
Set Conscience at a distance,
Passive obedience is a Joke,
A Jest is non resistance. (And this is Law etc.)

When Glorious Ann, became our Queen,
The Church of Englands Glory,
Another face 0f things was seen,
And I became a Tory:
Occasional Conformists base,
I Damn'd and Moderation,
And though the Church in danger was,
From such Prevarication. (And this is Law etc.)

When George in Pudding time came o'er,
And Moderate Men look'd big Sir,
My Principles I changed once more,
And so became a Whig Sir,
And thus Preferment I procur'd,
Frm our Faiths Great Defender,
And almost every day abjur'd,
The Pope and the Pretender (And this is Law etc.)

The Illustrious House of Hannover,
And Protestant Succession,
To these I lustily will swear,
Whilst they can keep possession.
For in my Faith and Loyalty,
I never once will falter,
But George, my Lawful king shall be,
Except the Times shou'd alter. (And this is Law etc.)

The war of the Austrian Succession was between 1740 and 1748, a confrontation in which Russia and Germany fought on opposite sides. Russia defeated Sweden and Prussia defeated Austria. They were on opposites sides again during the Seven Years war, 1756-1763 but when Tsar Peter 3rd rose to power, he signed the Treaty of Saint Petersburg, a peace contract between himself and the Prussian King, Frederick the Great. Then in another switch in 1771, 1793 and 1995, Prussia, Russia and Austria shared Poland/Lithuania between them. For a period, Poland was non-existent.

When the French Revolution resulted in the execution of the King, Russia and Prussia supported the new French regime during the French revolutionary wars and later, the Napoleonic Wars. There was a time when Austria, Russia and Prussia supported Napoleon in his violent dislike of Great Britain. But aha! Austria and Prussia then united with Russia and Britain in opposing Napoleon, (1813-1814). Russia became the most powerful country in Europe. It made its presence felt in the Concert of Europe, which included Britain, Austria, France and Russia but not Prussia.

The Concert of Europe was a group of European countries between 1814 and 1914, who decided to work together as an 'alliance', for the good of them all. The countries concerned were Britain, Austria, France (after the defeat of Napoleon) and Russia/Prussia (Prussia no longer being an independent country). So we had Lord Castlereagh, Britain's Foreign Secretary, Prince Klemenz von Metternich, the Austrian Chancellor and the Russian Czar Alexander 1st in 'concert'. The aims were laudable and could have been beneficial to Europe in its totality but the inevitable happened. There were disagreements and the Concert fell apart in the middle of the 19th century. However, there was an emergence in the 1920s, with more countries joining to form the 'League of Nations'.

The 1848 Revolutions did not involve Russia but the country suffered from an economic system that was rapidly failing the country, especially in the need to establish an efficient up-to-date army. Russia was beaten in the Crimean War, which itself had seen the end of the Concert of Europe. The Crimean War was fought by an alliance of Britain, Turkey, France and Sardinia, against Russia. Russia had tried to invade Romania, which at the time was under Turkish Control. It seems that Britain joined in this war for many reasons but mainly because there was concern that Russia may continue pushing into the Danube area and thence into Afghanistan and eventually into British India.

The Crimean War finished in 1855, with no lasting positive outcomes for any country. The story of the Crimean War is for another time and place but it is another part of the jigsaw of history that has led to my better understanding of the relationships between the countries, particularly of Germany and Russia and also the hostility that has inspired much the same unrest with the West, over the centuries. In the 1850s, the Russian Tsar, Nicholas the First, was the centre of the crisis of the Crimean War. Today in 2014, it is Vladimir Putin currently, with the conflicts with Ukraine.

So, continuing with this potted history, the 20th century brought confusing relations between the newly created states of the Weimar Republic and the Soviet Union. In fact, after the peace treaties that ended the First World War, both Germany and the Soviet Union found themselves outside the international system and so tended to move towards each other. In August 1939, these two states came to a major agreement, namely the Molotov-Ribbentrop pact. Poland was partitioned and Eastern Europe divided.

However, in the early years of the war, there were disputes as to new divisions of South East Europe, followed by the realisation that Slovakia was now under German influence. The Russian desire to have exclusive control in Romania, Bulgaria and Turkey was rejected by Berlin in November in 1940. Operation Barbarossa began in June 1941 and Soviet armies were captured or destroyed and the Germans actually reached the gates of Moscow in December.

Stalin retaliated by forging relationships with Britain and the United States. Germany, defeated by both the Soviet Union and the Western allies, pointed the way to the occupation and the partition of Germany. There were now tensions between the Western allies and the USSR, as to what would become of Germany after the 1939-45 war, particularly in the light of the Soviet's refusal to include the Soviet zone of Germany and indeed, the Soviet sector that lay within Berlin.

The immediate future of Germany had been agreed at the conferences at Yalta in February 1945 and at Potsdam, at Schloss Cecilien, in July and August 1945. The Yalta Conference, sometimes known as the Crimea Conference (code-name Argonaut Conference), was held on February 4th-11th, 1945 and was the meeting of the governmental heads of the USA, UK and Soviet Union, Franklin D. Roosevelt, Winston Churchill, and the Premier of Russia, Joseph Stalin. This Conference was held at the Livadia Palace, near Yalta in the Crimea.

Crown Prince Wilhelm Hohenzollern, son of Kaiser Wilhelm had a country style manor house built by the Heiligen Lake between 1913 and 1917 and it was at Schloss Cecilien, that the Potsdam Conference (originally called the Berlin Conference of the Three Heads of Government of the USSR, USA and UK), was host to the Communist Party's General Secretary, Joseph Stalin, the UK Prime Minister, Winston Churchill (later, his place was taken by Clement Atlee) and President Harry S. Truman. These leaders met to make decisions as to what retributions should be meted out to the defeated Nazi Germany, which had surrendered on May 8th,1945, (ever after known as VE Day). At Potsdam, Germany had been split into four occupational zones west of the Oder-Neisse line for administrative purposes, during the period 1945-1949, Soviet, American, British and French. East of the Oder-Neisse line was under Polish and Soviet annexation.

In the first instance, France was not included in the apportioning of an occupational zone, as its role had been a minor one, thus far, in any negotiations. There was also a feeling that the historical differences between France and Germany, could present communication difficulties.

It had been Charles de Gaulle who had insisted on a positive role for France after the war. In consideration of the part his country had played during the war as one of the Allied Powers, Britain and America decided to surrender small portions of their assigned zones to the French, along the border with France, with the Headquarters of the French military government being in Baden Baden. In addition, the Saargebiet, which was very important economically because of its large coal deposits, was enlarged and later, in 1947, it became the Saar Protectorate. It had been a region of South West Germany and had been contested between Germany and France because of the battle to control the coal.

After the First World War, the League of Nations assigned the administration of this Saar area to France but again it went back to the control of Germany, as a German province, in 1935. I have mentioned 'links' before, in the context of countries changing borders and the Saar is a good example, when the Protectorate became within the Control of France once again. Although an independent State, its economy was amalgamated within the economy of France. In my view, in having the virtual control of this valuable coal supply, the status of France may well have benefitted within the Occupied Zones. As far the Saar is concerned, this autonomy was rejected by the people themselves in 1957 and the region became once again, a state of West Germany. I have included this history of the Saar as an example of the information that I have researched recently and found to be enlightening and clarifying.

Berlin was a multinational area within the designated Soviet Zone but because of its importance as the capital city of Germany and with the added import of being the former headquarters of the Nazi Party, Berlin was jointly occupied by the Allied Powers and therefore, was also divided into four sectors.

That was the plan but in the closing weeks of fighting, American forces had pushed beyond these agreed boundaries, in some places as much as 200 miles. The line of contact between the Soviet and American Forces at the end of the hostilities, was only temporary. After a short period, in which they held areas that had been assigned to the Soviet Zone, American forces withdrew in the first months of 1945.

There was a general feeling at the time, that speculating on this event as to possible outcomes, was the crucial move that persuaded the Soviet Union to allow British, American and French Forces into their pre-designated zones in Berlin. Sir Frank Roberts, speaking at an RAF Historical Society Seminar, *(The Berlin Airlift 24th June, 1989)*, explained that he was Private Secretary to Ernest Bevin at that time and suggested that in the first year and a half after the war, anti-Communist Bevin did all he could to encourage the Americans and the British to work with the Russians.

In fact, he proposed a new 50 years alliance with the Russians and Truman, in America, was working along the same lines. However, the aims of the UK and America were not matched by

Russia, whose leaders had different ideas about the future. Later, In January 1947, Britain and America joined their two 'zones' into one, namely 'Bizonia'. (Bi-Zone). Nevertheless, the aims of the Big Powers had a very different purpose and whereas Britain and America looked towards the rebuilding of Germany, Stalin's plans involved the destruction of the whole country.

By July 1945, in an un-naturally quick time, to my thinking, the Red Army was in control of the Baltic States, Poland, Czechoslovakia, Hungary, Bulgaria and Romania. In fact, Stalin had already created a communist government in Poland, giving reasons to the effect, that he was creating defensive measures against future attacks and convinced himself that it was a legitimate move on the part of the Soviets. The citizens of these countries were not convinced and left these countries in their thousands, as refugees.

By this time, Roosevelt had died (April 12th 1945) and Truman was the new President of the USA. In the UK, the Prime Minister was now Clement Atlee, who had beaten Winston Churchill in the recent election. During the war Roosevelt had remained steadfast in his refusal to believe that Stalin was a danger and fully believed that given the opportunity to work together he and Stalin could work together, ' for a world of democracy and peace'.

Churchill on the other hand, since the 1940s, had believed that Stalin was a, 'devil-like tyrant, leading a vile system'. Truman thought differently than his predecessor and after the war, the two great powers of the UK and the USA showed unity and relationship, which was pivotal in the re-shaping of Germany.

In June 1948, the Western Allies went ahead with the reform of currency in their own zones of Germany and within their own sectors of Berlin, replacing the Reichmarks with Deutschmarks.

You can imagine that the Soviets in retaliation, made more and more difficulties, especially with all transport communications. The Freight trains that would normally have been bringing supplies into the city, were stopped, followed quickly by the passenger trains. The important autobahn between Hanover and Berlin was closed off, so that the Allied zones and the western sectors of Berlin, were completely cut off from each other. Russia retaliated on 23rd June 1948, by closing all access to Berlin by road and railway from the Western zones of Germany. The Russians for some time had been the main suppliers of electricity and coal to Berlin but these vital commodities now ceased. It was reported that Berlin had reserves of power that would last only three weeks.

Therefore the only way now left to reach Berlin was by air, using the corridors which had been settled in November 1945, by the four occupying powers.

There was an enormous possibility of a war situation but in the event, the Allies made plans for a complicated and comprehensive Airlift, with the aim of keeping the two million West Berliners fed and with power, in fact keeping them alive. This was a huge ambition because at its initiation, food, petrol and fuel in the Berlin stocks were estimated to have lasted only from two or three weeks. I understand that the city needed 1800 to 2000 tons of food each day. Fully laden Dakotas could hold about 2.5 tons.

Air Commodore R.N (Rex) Waite had been the man in charge of the disarming of the Luftwaffe at the end of the war. He had seen the difficulties now being faced by the German refugees, the very poor conditions of the people, the now inadequate infrastructure in Germany and the plight of all the servicemen and women who had been disbanded from their units. He decided to further his stay in Germany as the Air Section Chief for the Combined Services Division of the Control Commission for Germany, which was based in Berlin. In a letter to Air Commodore Gardener in 1947, he wrote,

'This is the most interesting job I have ever had. We are the leaders in all matters for the western zones and my team of free nations are constantly against the machinations of the Soviet.

The latter are constantly making difficulties, so that the Western Powers shall find it awkward to maintain themselves in Berlin and recently they have intensified their campaign.'

(compiled by Romilly Waite, for paper, 'Rex Waite', on 'The British Berlin Airlift Association' website)

It became the work of Air Commodore Waite to organise the requirements for the 2,200,000 citizens of West Berlin. In fact, two days before the Blockade was finally in place, he had informed RAF Transport Command that in all probability, an airlift in some form or other would be necessary. On the 23rd June, 1948, he submitted a draft plan for a joint British and American airlift system to provide sustenance for the besieged Berliners, to Major General Herbert, the Commander of the British Sector of Berlin. Herbert initially felt that it was not a viable plan but after much hard work from Rex Waite, he agreed to show the details to General Brian.K.Robertson, the British Military Governor. Robertson agreed to the plan enthusiastically and showed it to General Clay, the American Military Governor. Anthony Mann *(Comeback:Germany 1945-52, pub. Macmillan 1981)* wrote that:

'An impression has since grown up and with constant repetition, has become almost an article of faith, that the original project for the Berlin Airlift was American and that it derived essentially from General Clay himself. But, although the basic plan would never have stood a chance without Clay's enthusiastic backing, it was in fact the work of an RAF officer, Air Commodore R.N.Waite, at that time, Director of the Air Branch of the British Control Commission in Berlin.'

I have quoted Mann, as he is more authoritative than I about the politics of the day and also I cannot better his words. Nevertheless, I have wondered why Rex Waite has not always been given the accolade that he so deserved and that in so many books and even media documentaries, it is the Americans and General Clay in particular, who have been accredited with the success of the Airlift.

Sir John Tusa, introducing a seminar on the Berlin Airlift (Wednesday 4th June,1989) pointed out that, 'the all-important matter of political will and the way in which that political will came from Ernie Bevin *(U.K.Foreign Secretary)* – and without that political will, would any of the rest of it have happened?'

Looking back over the vast chasm of the years since that time, I would rather accept that all those concerned in the saving of Berlin, almost assuredly Germany and possibly the rest of Europe, deserve the recognition and the accolades, whatever nationality.

The West had established three air corridors, which connected the western zones of Germany to Berlin. In the first instances, supplies were sent to the besieged garrisons of the West, followed closely by the dropping of food for the civilian population of Berlin.

The British had a further problem in that the runway at Gatow airfield, which was then the only airfield in operation in the British zone, was having major repairs. Nevertheless, the British operation started, when two Dakota Squadrons, numbers 53 and 77 based at Waterbeach, were repositioned at Wunstorf.

The first Dakota flew to Gatow at 0600 hours on 28th June 1948. The six remaining Dakota squadrons followed soon after. On July 29th, the RAF Dakotas moved to Fassburg, which had to have a complete renovation for Operation 'Plainfare'. In fact, the new hardstanding was completed in just seven days. The RAF stayed at Fassburg until 22nd August, when the American aircraft took over, with the RAF aircraft being transferred to Lubeck, which again, had to have extensive improvements, including a lengthened concrete runway. The extension of the runway began on the 26th June 1948, extending the original inadequate length to 1800 metres and its width to 60 metres, the necessary size for the duties it now had to provide.

As I know to my cost (see Chapter, 'Life at the Camp'), the boundary of the Soviet Zone was only a mile or two from the eastern boundary of Lubeck airfield, which meant that extra care was required for all the RAF Operations. The last Dakota flight from Lubeck, 73,705 tons, to be precise, took place on September, 22nd,1949. Frank Stillwell, now sadly deceased, the then Chairman of The British Berlin Airlift Association, wrote in the Newsletter of

February 2003, that on that last Dakota flight, there was an inscription, Psalm,21, Verse 11.

'For they intended evil against thee, they imagined a mischievous device which they were unable to perform.'

Frank also recounted his experiences at Lubeck and graphically described how on the 26th April 1945, three Arado AR-234 jet reconnaissance aircraft were the last German aircraft to land at Lubeck before the end of the Second World War. He understood that Lubeck Airfield was the first to be captured by the RAF Regiment, whilst the war was still in operation. On the 6th May 1945, No 24 Wing took over as the occupying force. From August 1948 onwards, 70 RAF Dakotas were transferred from Fassburg, resulting in one hundred flights each day, to Berlin. On the return flights, the aircraft returned approximately 50,000 refugees. In the main, they were children and the elderly requiring medical help in West Germany. After the time of the Airlift, Lubeck Airport was developed as a commercial airport.

On October 5th, the civilian Dakotas that had worked alongside the RAF since Wunstorf, were sent to Fuhlsbuttel, in order to ease the situation of too many aircraft in too small a space and the RAF Yorks, (4-engined) aircraft, which had been gathered in from all over the world, had then been flown to Wunstorf and had started their Airlift operations on July 3rd. Eventually there were eight York squadrons. On 5th July, Sunderland flying boats flew from the Elbe, near Hamburg, to Lake Havel, near Berlin.

Altogether, 26 civil charter companies were involved, with many and varied types of aircraft. Berlin had a second airfield, Templehof, which was under the jurisdiction of the Americans, though was still used by the British and equally, Gatow was available to the Americans. On October 15th, BAFO and USAFE established a joint Airlift Task Force (CALTF) at Wiesbaden. On 1st November the first Hastings C.Mk aircraft from 47th Squadron was present in Tegel, when a new airfield, in the French Sector, was opened. It had been built for the sole purpose of relieving the amount of traffic from Templehof and Gatow. The whole airfield had taken only four months in August 1948, to build from scratch.

As a point of interest, the origin of the name of Templehof Airport came from the original use of this site by the Knights Templar in medieval Berlin. Later, the Prussian forces used the land as a parade field and then it was used by the German Forces from 1720 until the start of the First World War. The airport halls and numerous buildings were purported to have become the gateway to Europe and as symbol of Hitler's world capital, to be known as 'Germania'.

Sir Norman Foster a British architect, described the area as the 'mother of all airports' and in fact, the main building of the airport is supposedly the 20th largest building on earth. The airport had its heyday between 1938 and 1939 when the Second World War intervened.

Soviet forces took Templehof in the Battle of Berlin on April 24th, 1945, in the closing days of the war, with Templehof's German commander committing suicide rather than carry out orders to blow up the base. As had been agreed at Yalta and reiterated by the Potsdam agreement, Templehof was turned over to the second armoured division of the American army as part of the American occupation zone of Berlin. 'Operation Vittles' began in earnest on 26th June, for the USAF, when Douglas C-47 'skytrains', carried 80 tons of food into Templehof, then soon to be augmented by the United States Navy and Royal Air Force cargo aircraft, as well as several independent airlines.

The allies created a unified command between the separate US and British airlift efforts, on 15th October 1948, to ensure the increased safety and co-operation, with Major General William H.Tunner, in charge of the combined Airlift Task Force. The last airlift transport touched down at Templeof on the 30th September 1949. Many years later, in 2008, the sad decision was made to close the airfield. For many years, including 2014 there has been a ceremony at the Airlift Memorial, still to be seen at Templehof, where representatives from all the countries involved, meet together to remember that momentous year and place flower wreaths to remember all those who died.

The Author at the Gatow Memorial 2003

A letter in the BBAA Newsletter on October 31st 2008, from Baerbel.E.Simon, who directs the Cold War Museum in Berlin, informed us that Templehof had 85 years of continuous operation, and was one of the oldest airports in the world. She explained that as a piece of history, the Airport had divided the Berliners in their support or otherwise, of keeping the Airport open.

'The West Berliners still see Templehof as a symbol of liberty and for thousands of eastern refugees, Templehof was the gateway to freedom too. Many East Berliners see the Airport as a symbol of a divided city that lasted for so long and a turning point in the Allied-Soviet relations that spelled the birth of the Cold War.'

She explained also that there was now a project to move all the Berlin air traffic to one airport, Berlin Brandenburg International (BBI), which was then scheduled to open in 2011, to be constructed on the current Schoenefeld Airport.

At the time, the opening of the BBI was to close yet another airfield, namely Tegel. However in the event, (now 2014) Schoenefeld, though open to some flights, is in a state of flux and Tegel is therefore still receiving most of the civil flights bound for Berlin.

Baerbel concluded her letter by voicing her sadness that such an icon of the aviation world, such as Templehof, was going to disappear. In fact the Airfield did close as suggested (2011). I still remember it, many years after the Airlift, when it was the home of Lufthansa, the Civil Airline, on which I flew on occasion.

Airbases, plus the aircraft, that were used, during the Berlin Airlift

The bases used in the Allied Sectors:
Gatow - British Sector
Tegel- French Sector
Templehof- American Sector
Havel Lake- British Sector (RAF Sunderland Flying Boats until December 1948)

Bases used in the British zone:

Wunstorf- Dakotas ,25th June 1948, then 4-engined Yorks to the end of the airlift
Fassberg- Dakotas from 29th July 1948 and then USAF C54 Skymasters
Lubeck- Dakotas from 29th August 1948 to the end of the airlift.
Celle- used by USAF C54 Skymasters from 16th December 1948
Schleswigland- RAF Hastings from 11th of November 1948 to October 1949

Hamburg Finkenwerder - RAF Sunderland flying boats from 5th July to 16th December 1948
Hamburg Fuhlsbuttel- British Civil Airlift aircraft from 5 October 1948 to 15 August 1949

Bases used in the American zone:

Frankfurt-Rhein/Main- used by USAF C54 Skymasters
Weisbaden- used by USAF C54 Skymasters

Sir Peter Masefield, the then Chief Executive of British European Airways, in a letter to the 'Daily Telegraph', May 18th 1998, described his responsibility for the co-ordination of the 103 'widely assorted aircraft', contributed by 20 civil airlines, including BEA and BOAC (British Overseas Airways Corporation). Also involved were five flying boats.

'In just over a year from July 27th, 1948, the civil aircraft flew 88,000 tons of supplies – including nearly all of the liquid fuel – to Gatow airport and the flying boat base. The US Air Force provided 441 aircraft and the RAF 147 - and we should not forget that some of the crews were loaned by the Air Forces of Australia, Canada and New Zealand and South Africa. In all 2.5 million tons of food and other supplies were delivered.' *(Sir Peter Masefield, 1998).*

In 2005, now living in the West Country, I heard that three of the civilian personnel lived in the locality and after contacting them, I was delighted when they gave me details about particular services to the Airlift. Sadly, now in 2014, all three have died but their stories are worth recalling.

Richard Swale worked on the Airlift with his friend Flt.Lt G.H.Leonard who flew Hastings to Gatow, though based in the UK. On one occasion he flew freight to Gatow, knowing full well that on this particular 'round trip', there was no possibility of refuelling. They delivered the cargo, and then realised that the aircraft was running out of fuel and radioed Frankfurt for emergency refuelling. Frankfurt refused the request. Flt.Lt.Leonard insisted on landing anyway and in defiance of the order, the aircraft did land and they eventually obtained the necessary fuel to get them back to the U.K. and safety.

Michael Turner served in the RWF stationed at Abingdon where he was attached to Transport Command. His flights to Berlin were in the capacity of radio expert, absolutely essential, for receiving and transmitting the many commands that were made during a journey.

Bill Blackett was a civilian who was based in Berlin and was there after the cessation of the Airlift at the same time as Germany, was living in a divided geographical and political situation. He stayed in a small hotel for two separate periods and in the aftermath of the Airlift, flew Dakotas up until 1953.

The flying was always between Berlin and Hannover or Hamburg and his log book records that for both of the periods in which he spent flying hundreds of hours, he was ferrying German refugees attempting to escape from the Russians. The operation was called, 'Air Charter, Sub-Charter, Berlin Refugee Flights.' He flew three or four round trips each day, with the flying being very concentrated, comprising of many more take-offs and landings than normal. They were briefed never to stray more than a mile or two off track, as the Russians were alleged to be very 'trigger happy'.

I have included the story of Bill Blackett, as an example of the years after the Airlift. There was no nice tidy line drawn underneath the Airlift in 1949. The problems continued and in fact there are still many problems unresolved today.

The weather in Germany during those first months of the Airlift, was wet and uncomfortable and the aircraft due to land would often find themselves approaching in deep mud. Manpower was very short from both ends of the flights and in addition to using German civilians, vital help was given by British Commonwealth crews from Australia, New Zealand and South Africa.

The name given to the British operation changed many times, 'Knicker' and 'Carter Paterson', then re-named 'Plainfare' on 19th

July, 1948. 'Vittles' was the Americans codeword. On the whole, 'Blockade' and the 'Airlift' seemed to be the most favoured and recognisable, certainly to me, at the time and ever since. The difficulties that were faced were tremendous. For instance, Wunstorf, one of the British bases was very small and was not equipped to any degree for a difficult and essentially life-saving operation as was being launched. On top of which, the poor weather at that time was not conducive to an easy and straightforward venture.

The electrical systems of the aircraft did not take kindly to the everlasting rain either. In Gatow, there were occasions when the aircraft could not fly at all, until the runways had been cleared of the vast quantities of water that had accumulated with the incessant rainfall.

Even so, by the middle of July, the RAF were handling 840 tons of goods destined to alleviate the miseries of the inhabitants of Berlin. The return journeys were used to fly passengers out from Berlin and also loads sent by the remaining manufacturers, who needed to get their goods to the outside world, to ensure what little profit was possible in such difficult times. More to the point, they needed to keep their businesses as active as possible, so that when freedom was restored, the firms were ready to take their place in the manufacturing and commercial world. With an agreement by the Americans, the total responsibility for flying out these substantial quantities of goods, sacks of mail and service as well as civilian passengers, was taken by the British aircraft, some 35,843 tons of materials and 131,436 people.

Much has been written in detail about the airlift manoeuvres, the aircraft used, the loads that were dropped, the hazards faced by the pilots, the vital role of the ground staff, particularly those who had to keep patching up the deteriorating 'planes, with all the bravery and downright hard work of all the personnel involved. There were crashes on all sides. Even so, there were remarkably few, considering the amount of traffic in the skies at the same time.

However, the one about which I know most, is the accident to Dakota KN 491 at Spitzberg bei Schattin on the night of the 24/25th of January, 1949. The pilot Ervin John Eddy and I became friends many years later when he returned to his home in Camborne, Cornwall, a few miles from Bodmin, where I now live. We were also members of the British Berlin Airlift Association, formed in 1994, which gave us the opportunity to return to Germany for the yearly celebrations at Templehof.

John died in 2013 and to the end, never forgot the crash and sadly, the people who died. In addition, the severed nerve in his shoulder, which was one of his many serious injuries, rendered his arm less and less useful as he grew older.

He gave me a copy of the accident report, for my use. The crew consisted of the pilot, Ervin, (always known as John) Eddy, the navigator L.Senior and the signaller, J.E Grout. Their unit was the No. 1 Parachute and Gliding Training School, at Royal Air Force Upper Heyford. The crew was detailed to take part in Operation Plainfare and were ordered to fly as passengers to RAF Oakington on 7th January 1949 and to further proceed as passengers from Oakington on 8th January to RAF Lubeck for flying duties on the airlift. John reported that on the night of the 24th/ 25th of January, 1949, the crew were ordered to carry the normal load, using briefed SOP (Standard Operating Procedures) along the northern corridor.

The flight was apparently uneventful and they landed successfully at RAF Gatow. Their instructions for the return flight were unusual, in that the proposed night journey had as the 'load', twenty two passengers, comprising of 14 ladies, 5 children and 3 men. The aircraft was normally used to carry troops, so that the accommodation consisted of campus bucket seats along each side of the fuselage, with the appropriate number of safety straps. Believe me, I know all about that delight, as I also had to fly to Lubeck from Buckeburg and the lack of seats, the paper pasted over the windows and the low-flying height, changed the colour of my face to a very sickly green.

John said that the passengers were briefed on the operation of the straps and the quick release mechanism. The weather brief concerning the conditions of Lubeck, was of low cloud and westerly wind and when the 'plane left the central corridor, the crew were informed that the weather had worsened to a cloud base of 300 feet and the Babs, (Beam Approach Beacon System) was only being picked up at 1 mile. The crew was then instructed to start descending, using the radio compass in order to be at 300 feet, to do a visual circuit and landing. The pilot decided to turn towards the near field approach, using the radio compass to line up with the centre line of the runway in an individual final adjustment when they picked up the BABS.

It was unfortunate when turning, maintaining 300 feet, the aircraft hit some trees and crashed in the woods near Spitzberg bei Schattin. John was severely injured and knocked unconscious. The navigator sustained a minor injury to his hand but the signaller who was in the passenger compartment at the time, was fatally injured. John had many injuries and eventually was sent to Lubeck, thence to Hamburg, then evacuated by boat to Southampton, finally to a hospital in Ely. After two years convalescence, he returned to his duties. The navigator told how he removed the pilot from flames and with two passengers (Herr Zeidler and Herr Brandis (Polish), he went to Lubeck to get help.

The journey was not made easy by a stream and a bog and the Ratzeburg Lake, which was at the border of East and West Germany. They were forced back to the 'plane to await help and on the way back found a forester's cottage. Herr Luhr raised the alarm for some help. Eventually East German and Russian troops took all the passengers to Schonberg hospital. Apparently, they were all roughly cross-examined. One of the passengers reported that they were interrogated by the Russian authorities, who accused them of being spies but eventually they were released. Nothing apparently was heard of the Polish passenger (Herr Brandis) again.

A group from the BBAA (British Berlin Airlift Association), including John and myself, visited the area, many years later and saw the local hospital where the initial help was given. We laid a wreath in the forest. John also visited Herr Luhr's son, who told him sadly that after the crash, the Russians came to the forester's cottage the next day, firing rifles in the air and demanding the Englanders. This resulted in Herr Luhr suffering a fatal heart attack. There are always casualties in war, even in a Cold War. John never did recover emotionally or physically.

I watched so much and even took part in my small way in the vital work of the air traffic control. However, I am leaving the technicalities and the statistics to those who are far more expert than I. My intention in this small volume, is to chart my life during the Berlin airlift as an aircraftwoman, posted from a safe environment in the UK to a different world, certainly an unfamiliar country but also a whole battery of circumstances that that I did not understand.

Chapter 2 – The Start of My Journey

The start of my journey really took place in the year 1948, which became an important milestone in my life and a great influence on how I have viewed the world ever since. During the uncertain period after leaving school, I had trained as a singer, had worked on a newspaper and spent some time in a Senior Boys' school in Brighton as secretary and untrained teacher, a situation imposed on schools owing to the absence of the male teachers who had been called-up during the war.

The pressure was on for those of my age, to serve in the Forces and eventually I joined the RAF, the 'WAAF' as it was then for we women, the Women's Auxiliary Air Force, so no equality there! Later the name was changed to the Womens' Royal Air Force, after we had shown that the women were equally as valuable as the men! In the first instance, I was sent for Basic Training to Wilmslow, in Cheshire. The whole episode was a shock, from the train journey northwards, as I had seldom left the Home Counties, to being herded into a vast cavern of a room where I was given my uniform, which only fitted me, 'in parts'.

Sharing a billet was the next hurdle. I had been used to a room of my own and so, confronted with a long bare room with narrow bunks, covered in a rough blanket, it was not quite the comfort that I had assumed would be my lot. We were then issued with a sheet and a towel and a knife, fork and spoon and told to report to the canteen in thirty minutes. I thought that I may just have time for a warm comforting bath, which actually went through a state of metamorphosis into a cold wash in the communal wash room, where the showers gave forth warm water, only at specified times. I had six weeks at Wilmslow and learned to march and salute and importantly share the space with the other WAAFs. I also had to learn to roll my long hair round a stocking, so that it rested above my collar. Hair that appeared above the collar was destined for the hairdresser's scissors.

We had interviews as to our suitability for the duties available to us and prepare us for our future in the Service. Possibly because of my school experience and my propensity for administration, officer training was mentioned. I was still a very 'new girl' and not sufficiently convinced that the RAF was my ambition for a lifetime career, plus the fact that I was told that to enable officer training, I would have to commit to a much longer term of service and I was far from making that sort of decision. Two years seemed a very long time as it was and also I had been making tentative approaches with regard to future Teacher Training, encouraged by the Head of the School at which I had been working. In fact, I was offered a place at Wymondham Training College, whilst I was serving in the WAAF and naturally, it was not possible for me to accept the offer. It did strengthen my wish to follow that course of action in the future. In the event, after marriage and children, at a much later date, I did eventually attend Teachers' Training College. Nevertheless, I know now that my service life and experiences were invaluable to me.

At Wilmslow I was directed toward Air Traffic Control and I spent time at Bawdsey, in Suffolk, training on the RADAR system (Radio and Detection and Ranging). I was billeted in a magnificent building, Bawdsey Manor, the family home of Sir Roger Quilter, the composer. I was very impressed by this posting, as I had sung his songs many times at school and also during my singing training. The house was built by his father, Sir Cuthbert Quilter in the late 1890s. Sir Roger himself was born in Hove, Sussex and died in St. John's Wood, London at the age of 73, being then buried in the family vault in St. Mary's Church, Bawdsey.

We were able to enjoy the historic parkland as well as swimming in the Deben estuary. In 1936, Bawdsey Manor became a top secret research establishment for the Ministry of Defence and was used by Sir Robert Watson Watt and his team to develop radar technology. Later there was a chain of radar stations running along the south coast to help in the defence of Britain during World War II.

Today the old transmitter block, where we did our training is now a museum, which tells the story of Radar and of course how Bawdsey helped to win the Battle of Britain. I have visited the museum in more recent years, with mixed emotions. I felt proud that I had been involved in very important work at that time but sad as well, that technology, like life, is dynamic and moves on. Other techniques have overtaken the Radar that I knew. However, there is in fact a group, called Bawdsey Radar, which was formed by a group of local people in 2003, to preserve the transmitter block and thus preserve our very important history.

We had a Newsletter called the 'Express', described as the, 'Britain's Hottest Service Paper'. In fact it was four sides of a foolscap-sized piece of printer paper, of very poor quality. One edition was printed on Wednesday September 3rd, 1947 and the front page reported the astonishing news that several mines had been found on the beach, the very swimming beach that had provided much of our off-duty pleasure. The newspaper solemnly warned us that the beach was 'now out of bounds'. In the same issue, we were told that the NAAFI manageress had reported that in her opinion,

'Thefts of NAAFI cups were 'not excessive'. We are also told that the Fete and Fancy Dress Parade in which we joined with the local people, had been very successful. Several WAAFs, myself included apparently, paraded in our costumes and during the evening festivities, I sang a solo. I can neither remember the nature of the costume nor the song that I sang! The 'Express' reported all of the activities of the camp whether official, amusing or sad. Before the beach was closed to us, one of our lads drowned whilst bathing in the sea. We were shocked at his loss and the waste of a young life in such a pointless way.

I wonder how many of you remember Arthur Askey and Richard Murdoch, as much loved comedians during the Second World War. Their signature tune was allied to their fictional RAF station, 'Much Binding in the Marsh'. When I was stationed at Bawdsey Manor in Suffolk, the following skit on that song was published in our camp newsletter. (September 7th 1947)

Much Bawdsey
At Much Bawdsey in the Marsh
A clerk SD wrote home to his relations
At Much Bawdsey in the Marsh
It seems we have two examinations,
First we have an interim
Followed by a Trade Test by and by
I know I won't pass either, however hard I try,
But at least one thing is certain,
I'll pass my FFI!!
At Much Bawdsey in the Marsh.

At much Bawdsey in the Marsh,
The WAAFs are really most attractive
At Much Bawdsey in the Marsh
The airman on Service, are very active!
The instructors down at 5RS
Are men of great resource
And unless a regulation is quickly brought into force
They soon will find, that they have a wife on every Course!
At much Bawdsey in the Marsh

At much Bawdsey in the Marsh
It seems that we have got a lot of cricket
At Much Bawdsey in the Marsh
We use the Fire Squad to soak the wicket.
An AC.1 who batted well, began to shoot a line,
The CO overheard him and decided he was fine
He's a Sergeant now- he has been here since 1929
At much Bawdsey in the Marsh

(Clerk SD = Special Duties), (FFI=Free From Infection), (5RS=No. 5 Radar Station), (AC1=Aircraftman First Class), (are shooting a line=telling lies, exaggerating)

From Bawdsey, I took my newly learned information with me to my next postings at Stanmore and to Uxbridge, to train for Air Traffic Control. The feature that I noticed immediately in both the Control Rooms was, 'The RAF Operations Room Plotting Clock'. Officially I had been working as a 'plotter', so took an interest in the clock, especially as it had coloured triangles round the perimeter, which the plotters appeared to study closely and constantly. The work of the RAF Controllers and the plotters, was to receive all the information of aircraft, their altitude, bearing (direction) and the strength of any approaching aircraft. (especially pertinent in a war-time hostile situation).

This information was plotted onto the table and then the Officers in Charge would take appropriate action. Numerous messages had to be sorted, put in order of priority and disseminated extraordinarily quickly. It was tiring and worrying, as there was no room for error. This is where the Operations Room Clock came in, as a good way to sort the urgent from the non-urgent messages. All incoming reports would be colour coded with the colours of red, yellow or blue, depending on the actual time that they were received. These colour-indicated times were given according to the position of the minute hand on the Ops. clock. The triangles round the dial were in these three colours at five minute intervals. The colour that was indicated by the minute hand at the time that the message was received, would be the colour attached to the message and then plotted on the Operations Room map. It was confusing to follow at first but eventually we colour- coded automatically. It was said that that this system was successful in holding the control of the skies during the battle of Britain and future occasions.

The 'Ops' clock which dominated all Operation Rooms

I had been assigned to be Clerk SD, which meant Special Duties. I never quite knew why this was - but it did give me the chance to do some interesting jobs. The call came, just two days before my 21st birthday.

I was sent almost overnight to Germany. I felt really alone and very bewildered, as I knew nobody in the group at all and had no idea where I was heading. It was the first time I had been outside of England and cut off from communication with my parents. The homogenous group being posted to various German destinations, travelled at night and I do remember being herded onto the ferry at Harwich, with orders being shouted to us in the dark from faceless voices, whilst we shuffled miserably down countless stairs to the bottom level of the boat. The sea was very choppy and I felt very sick indeed, closeted as we were in this hot stifling deck. The nightmare continued when the necessity drove me to visit the 'head', (lavatory to the uninitiated) and I had to find my stumbling way along passages, still in the dark, to find a smelly cubicle that did nothing for my 'mal de mer', which did reach crisis point on the way back to my bunk.

We were put on a train which I later found was travelling across Belgium and eventually, with little comfort and even less refreshments or washing facilities, we arrived in Germany. We were in Hannover (Hanover), which meant little to me, except for the fact left over from my school days, that George 1st was a Hanoverian King. By this time, I had learned that there was a crisis, I knew that Berlin was under siege and that to enable people to survive, there was a need to fly food, coal and other necessities of life over German soil and drop them onto collection points in the city. My companions of the journey and I, were then put onto a gharry, an uncomfortable cross between a van and the box-like wheeled carriage that was usually to be found in India, thence to our differing units and as far as I know, we never met again.

There were very few going to Bad Eilsen, which I then learned was my destination and certainly I seemed to be the only female. I was escorted to a house, my bed was pointed out to me and I was left, still in the dark, as the other girls in the room were sleeping. That was a very low point for me! The next day was a voyage of discovery and as I was sent to work immediately, I had to learn very quickly the techniques of the job in hand, as well as the layout of the village, the facilities available to us and of course, the WAAFs, with whom I was now living. My corporal was a huge help and she even taught me how to iron my service shirts properly. The politics mainly eluded us at the time but during our lives since, many of the participants, including myself, have researched the causes and effects of the Berlin Airlift and realise now that the success of this whole operation was vital to the future of Germany, to Europe and in all probability, the UK.

I arrived on the 27th June, the first load was sent out from Wunstorf on the 28th June and I was 21 years old on the 29th June. My birthday was not celebrated at all, as work began in earnest. I have never found out how my father and my sister Audrey, managed to get a small parcel to Bad Eilsen but by using various channels, I received a book on opera from my sister, which is still in my possession and my father sent me a half sovereign on a chain, which I have worn constantly since that time and for me, it is a constant reminder of the Airlift

Wunstorf, Fassberg, Lubeck and Gatow (Berlin), were the chief operational airfields. The Americans had their own airfields including Templehof, which is still the scene of a remembrance service every year on May the 12th. I was interested to discover that after being designated on October 8th, 1923 by the Ministry of Transport, Templehof, in 1927, became the first airport in the world to have an underground railway station, now called ' Platz der Luftbrucke', after the Berlin Airlift. Sadly, though the airfield became a highly successful civil airport, housing the 20th largest building in the world, the whole site was scheduled for closure and although a referendum was held on 27th April, 2008 against the close-down, the low turn-out failed to reverse the decision to close. I was even more interested to find out that the site of the airport originally belonged to the Knights Templar in mediaeval Berlin, hence the name Templehof.

I was posted to Headquarters, BAFO (British Air Force Overseas), at Bad Eilsen and worked in ATCCBE (Air Traffic Control Centre) Operations room, in a wonderful building called the Kurmittal House. I was billeted in a house called 'Haus Waldblich' (by the wood) and the lawyer owner and his family were relegated to the basement.

I like to think that he was able to return to full ownership of his home, when the time came for us to return to the UK. Bad Eilsen is a municipality in the District of Schaumberg in Lower Saxony, about 11 kilometres south-west of Stadhagen and 13 kilometres southeast of Minden, a town that at the time housed one of our Army units. Bad Eilsen is very near to Buckeburg, with Hameln (Hamelin) and Hannover (Hanover), within easy distance and before the war, had been noted as a sulphur spa. It had been a regal resort, founded in 1780 by Juliane, the wife of the then ruling Count, Philipp Ernst Schaumburg-Lippe. It was however from the beginning of the 20th century that Bad Eilsen became 'the' fashionable place, where elegant society met to walk through the beautiful park and dine in the sophisticated atmosphere of the rich and famous.

I have a pre-war brochure of the spa and there is no doubt as to its beauty. Apparently, the sulphur springs contained the highest sulphur content of any in Central Europe, which had led to the most up-to-date and expensive, therapeutic equipment. Sulphuric 'sludge' has been used over the years for the mud baths, taken in these luxurious surroundings, for the relief of rheumatism. Bad Eilsen had also served a more serious purpose in that Kurt Tank's design for the Focke-Wulf jet 'plane, was accepted on 28th February, 1945 and at a meeting in that small but important village, Tank was told to plan for some mock-ups of the aircraft and to oversee its full production. The first flight was planned for May 1945 but completion had not taken place when the British troops captured the Focke-Wulf facilities.

I also have a copy of a photograph showing a rally in aid of the Third Reich, with crowds cheering and many flags soaring above the trees.

Years later, in fact in the 1990s, I went back for a visit and the small village had now turned into a much larger town with supermarkets and bus services, whereas it had been isolated, with very few shops and where people skied in the winter and walked in the summer. At first I could not find the huge buildings which were prominent in 1948 and housed the treatment rooms. Eventually I found the park and by now surrounded by trees, I found the original spa site and knew that I was there mainly because of the familiar smell of 'bad eggs'. The 'coat of arms' of Bad Eilsen, is a semi-circle of pillars in which a source of sulphuric water disgorges itself into a well.

I understand that the spa has now re-opened after a space of 70 years or so. The bygone luxury did not extend to we 'erks' of course. ('erks' were the newest recruits and the lowest ranks). The Badehof, formerly the Town Hall, was used for our headquarters and soon lost its splendour. The daily routine of an Air Force Station did not lend itself to marble, glass and velvet.

Strictly speaking, Bad Eilsen was not an operational headquarters, we had no airfield, no hoe girls worked there plotting 'planes, as I had expected. It was the policy headquarters, making decisions that co-ordinated rather than led. We RAF personnel called our room, the 'ops' room nevertheless and spent much time, receiving and passing on messages intended to instruct and direct. Bernard Maeder, a member of the Bad Eilsen Reunion (a UK Veteran's Association), worked in the A.T.C.C.B.E. building in the Kurmittel House as the supervisor from 1954-1955, following which, the unit moved to Hannover after the second TAF (Tactical Air Force), transferred to Munchen Gladbach. He was kind enough to send me a sketch that he had made of the Movements area, in which I worked, mainly in the Amendments and State of the Airfields room.

I remember vividly the enclosed raised glass area, which gave the Controller, a wide vision over the whole room. Opposite the door to this room was the Signals Traffic room where the signallers and teleprinters worked in the sending and receiving of messages. My to-be husband, as a 'Sparks', worked in this room and very often sent messages that I had forwarded to him. Air Traffic Control techniques and all the equipment used in 1948 were quite crude, compared to the high sophistication used today, in 2014. Even I, at the time, realised that the different types of aircraft used, especially those which had often been hasty additions to the 'fleet' as an emergency, had their own idiosyncrasies, even to flying at different speeds.

Drawing by Jack of the teleprinter used by him throughout the Airlift

Back-tracking somewhat, it may be useful to understand the importance of Bad Eilsen and its very real involvement in the Airlift. In the last few weeks of the war, RAF Squadrons in the TAF (Tactical Air Force), arrived in Germany alongside the 21st Army Group, led by Field Marshall Montgomery. TAF had been trained and equipped to work closely with those occupied in the ground war and now, at the end of the war, found themselves in a different position altogether, that of being an occupying power. Germany of course, was by now, occupied by the allies and TAF had to appreciate its new role. In July 1945, there was a new organisation formed, the British Air Force of Occupation (BAFO). BAFO was still to be on a partnership basis with the Army. The RAF HQ, being based at Bad Eilsen, meant that it was very near to Bad Oyenhausen, the HQ of the British Army of the Rhine. With Sir William Sholto Douglas in command, it was the task of BAFO to support BAOR and also to police the British Zone of Occupation. By the end of 1947, the original BAFO squadrons in various airfields, had been reduced to ten, mainly for economy measures. The remaining 10 squadrons were based at three airfields, Wunstorf, Gutersloh and Wahn, all being under the operational control of the Air Headquarters in Bad Eilsen.

Well after these events, taking part in a seminar on the Airlift, chaired by John and Ann Tusa, Sir Kenneth Cross described how he arrived at Headquarters, BAFO in January 1947, to take up the post of Group Captain Operations. BAFO was formed in 1945 from the 2nd TAF, not without problems because nobody in the BAFO headquarters, even the station commanders, had been in the 2nd TAF. Sir Kenneth reminded his audience that after the war all the establishments had been reduced in personnel, so HQ was not in a good situation to embark on an operation of which little was known.

'We had two roles in BAFO, air co-operation with the Army and the occupational role in which my AOC was responsible to the military governor General Robertson.' (RAF Historical Society Seminar, 'The Berlin Airlift, 1948-1949'), 1998.

He went on to explain that the headquarters was actually in two hotels, not ideal but adequate. His experiences make for very good reading and very enlightening for one in my position, now seeing the situation in retrospect and more to the point, actually having worked in one of those hotels.

Buckeburg, our nearest town, had a small airfield, which had been built in 1946 as a RAF Station, serving the Headquarters of the Royal Air Force in Germany, at Bad Eilsen. During the Airlift it was one of many airfields, which carried out many supply flights to Berlin. Much of our work dealt with Buckeburg, especially I remember, civilian passengers from Berlin. I flew twice from there myself, once to Lubeck to collect some information and once to the UK, when I had a short leave. The British Forces Joint Headquarters (JHQ) was built in Rheindahlen in 1954 , which meant that at the end of the 1950s, Buckeburg airfield was closed. I understand that in January 1960, the German School of Army Aviation moved to Buckeburg and now this Air Base is used for the instruction of flying and non-flying personnel, focussing on helicopters.

I have long wondered what the actual connection was between HQ Bad Eilsen and 'The Schloss' (Palace) at Buckeburg. To me, at the time, we seemed to perform much the same functions. Recently (July 2104) I was given some vital and most enlightening information from Juergen Balke, now a member of the Bad Eilsen Reunion. I had put the question to the Chairman Geoff Lipscombe, as to whether he had any members who had worked at the Schloss at the time of the Airlift and Juergen who now lives in Wunstorf, has been kind enough to inform me that during the Berlin Airlift, the numbers of available 'planes were limited and as well as Groups 46 and 47 and 48, the decision was made to involve the support of further bases in the British Zone.

'This meant a lot of additional work and RASO and FASO organisation for transport, loading and unloading. The Army were involved. These works could not be handled by HQ BAFO in its present strength and structure. Therefore it was decided to build up a new Headquarters near to Bad Eilsen. This was established in the Schloss, Buckeburg, which housed Headquarters Unit 46 Group.'

He described that from its beginning on the 22nd September 1948, this Group's responsibilities consisted of signals, navigation, air movements and aircraft control branches. The AOC 46 Group was responsible to the AOC (Air Officer Commanding), BAFO, with full control during the Airlift. However in 1949, Buckeburg was considered no longer suitable for the ever growing tasks and duties, so the HQ was transferred to Luneburg.

I personally, found the situation very confusing at the time. As far as I was aware, I effected the same jobs and procedures right to the end of my tour at the conclusion of the airlift in May, 1949. Juergen suggested that Air Traffic Control was still necessary for the movements of USAF, particularly aircraft that were operating from Celle and Fassburg and also for all the 'planes not immediately involved in the Airlift but were on important duties, both for the Armed Forces and for civilian needs.

Very soon after I had arrived at my new station, I became curious as to the more recent past of Bad Eilsen. I found that another role, amongst many, had been played out in the village between the pre-war time of the mud baths and the arrival of the RAF and then we 'Airlifters', soon after the end of the war. Bad Eilsen had been chosen to act as a 'baby farm', for their production of perfect Aryan children for Hitler's ideal Germany. Flaxen-haired mädchen were able to live in comfort, provided they produced a child yearly, from the 'stud' of equally 'pure' young men.

Today, these 'Lebensborn' (which means 'spring of life'), mainly live in Germany but are unsure as to their parentage or the nature of their true nationality. The Lebensborn project was one of the most frightening and very secret, Nazi programmes. It was created by Heinrich Himmler on December 12, 1935. The aims of this terrifying society was to establish the opportunity for racially pure women to give birth to a child in secret, which was then given to the SS organisation, following which, arrangements would be made for the child's education and possible adoption. The racially pure men required, usually SS officers or members of the Luftwaffe, were there only for the conception.

From 1939, Lebensborn policy included the kidnapping of children considered racially perfect, from many of the Eastern occupied countries. The SS took the children by force, who were then sent to a Lebensborn centre to become 'Germanised' and pressure was applied to erase their parents and their former lives, from their memories. Many children came from Poland and Czechoslovakia and if they tried to resist in any way, they would be sent to special children's camps and then later, to extermination centres.

By 1946, it was thought that well over 250,000 children were kidnapped. In my research on this subject, I found that roughly 25,000 only were found after the war and were allowed to go back to their families. There were cases of course where children wanted to stay with their adopted family and really believed that they were pure Germans. Now, in the 21st century, many of the Lebensborn, now in their sixties, have met together to ask questions about their births and lives and to try to trace their roots. There is a sense of shame endemic among them and far from being the rulers of the world, as the Nazis had envisaged, they still feel ostracised and belonging nowhere.

As a postscript to this information, a member of the Bad Eilsen Reunion, an Association which includes all those stationed at Bad Eilsen over all of its operational years, described in a recent Reunion 'Gazette' (2014), how he had been a member of the RAF Riding Team at Buckeburg in 1955. He tells of a RAF riding display for the people of Buckeburg, especially including the younger riders, both British and German, who had been having lessons at the school. One of the riders in the display was a German lad, with blond hair and a very good rider. The writer of this article asked the young man as to the whereabouts of his parents, I should think, assuming that they were in the audience.

Henry Bohne, the German riding instructor said, very firmly, 'That will do Mr.Cook. Leave it'. Later he explained that the lad was 'one of Hitler's children'. He then went on to explain that Bad Eilsen had been used as a 'baby factory', with two programmes. The top one – the Superior Race – were looking for fair haired, blue-eyed children who would grow up to hold all the 'top' jobs. Another group would boost the German population which had been depleted because of the massive deaths in the two world wars. When asked what had happened to the Superior Race babies, Henry Bohne described how they had been placed with selected families and the birth mothers were encouraged to have yet more babies. Bad Eilsen was only one of several 'baby farms' across the country. Mr Cook felt very sorry for these children and of course, this particular lad.

There was yet another group of people for whom we felt enormous sympathy. They were the vast numbers of children who roamed the countryside completely stateless, without care, homes, food, clothing or money. There were German children but also many from Poland and Czechoslovakia, in fact all the countries that had been disrupted and invaded by Germany and Russia. Particularly since the end of the war, they had no home to which to return. Such a group of children were camped in a village called Obernkirchen just a few miles from Bad Eilsen. Obernkirchen is a small town overshadowed by the 'Buckeburg', a hill range in the Weser Uplands.

The village itself overlooked the expanse of the old county of Schaumberg Lippe, now the District of Schaumberg, with the town of Buckeburg at its feet. Often, the children would be seen, searching in our dustbins for any remnants of food. Later, the village became very famous as the home of a childrens' choir, who travelled worldwide entertaining with their delightful singing. Their most popular song, 'I like to go a-wandering', became a hit in the 1950s.

However when I knew Obernkirchen in the 1940s, the children were far from being happy. They certainly wandered – in search of food and shelter. I remember their splayed feet, as most of them had no shoes to wear. They became part of the army of displaced people who had no accepted homeland. I do remember looking at the church in the village, in which they took shelter, which was damaged and neglected since organised religion had been banned during the war. I read a newspaper many years later, which told of the re-opening of the churches and Obernkirchen was one of them. The village itself also revived and is now a pleasant community.

Also, recently (2014), I discovered that there was a Jewish community in Obernkirchen, with their peak population in the 16th century. In 1861 there were 91 Jews left in the village and by 1933, only 42 remained. Most had worked as peddlers or merchants or butchers. A proper synagogue had been built in 1847 but in 1938 the community was dissolved and on the night of the Pogram, the synagogue was destroyed. There were many 'Pograms' – Violent Riots – but the most significant one was the Kristallnacht of 1938, in which 91 Jews were either killed or arrested, with many sent to concentration camps. 1000 synagogues were burned, with 7000 Jewish businesses damaged or utterly destroyed. Seven Jews from Obernkirchen were sent to Buchenwold, the concentration camp.

In 1944, the last of the community were deported. Sadly too, 16 had perished in the Shoah, being the Hebrew word for 'catastrophe'. The 'calamity', in this context, stood for the Holocaust, which was the Nazi Genocide of the Jewish people. As late as 1969, the cemetery was desecrated, a dreadful act, which was somewhat ameliorated in 1988 when a memorial stone was erected at the site of the synagogue, now a car park. For me this history begged several questions as to whether all, or some, of the children that I saw, scrambling in our dustbins at Bad Eilsen, were in fact Jewish , whether they were displaced because of their religion and importantly what happened to them. Did they find security, a home and a future?

Perhaps, in 2014, I found one explanation in the words of Susan Silas, an American/Hungarian writer .*(Susan Silas-Wikipaedia)*

'One of the folk songs I remember from my childhood in America is, 'The Happy Wanderer'. The song was composed in Germany after the Second World War, perhaps in an attempt to fill the void created, when the folk songs handed down for generations became associated with National Socialism. The song was composed by Friederich Wilhelm Moller and was called, 'Mein Vater war ein Wandersmann' or 'Der Frohliche Wanderer'. It was broadcast on BBC radio during the year I was born and became an instant hit.'

Mein Vater war ein Wandersmann
Und mire seckt's auch im Blut
Drum wandr'ich flott, so lang ich kann
Und schwenke meinen Hut.

Faleri, felara, faleri,
Falera ha ha ha ha ha ha ha
Faleri, FaleraValeri, Valdera
Und schwenke meinen Hut.
(Refrain)

I love to go a-wandering
Along the mountain track
And as I go, I love to sing
My knapsack on my back.

Val-deri, Val-dera
Valdera-ha-ha-ha-ha-ha ha ha
Valeri, Valdera
My knapsack on my back.

Four more verses follow and the German and English lyrics do not always match but the general idea was there, to create the feeling of happiness and freedom. The last English version epitomises the intended meaning of the song:

Oh, may I go a-wandering
Until the day I die!
Oh, may I always laugh and sing,
Beneath God's clear blue sky!

Susan Silas wrote, that the Obernkirchen Children's choir was composed mainly of German orphans, 'making an arresting impression and solving the problem of Nazi parentage'.

She thought about this 'clean' folk song, when she heard Franz Suchomel sing the song that he claimed the Jews were forced to memorize when they arrived at Treblinka. 'The inmates were treated in the most unspeakable ways, most dying in Horrific circumstances. In some ways, learning this song was the, 'unkindest cut of all'. After completing the song, Franz said with some pride, 'That is an original. No Jew knows how to sing that any more'.

Treblinka
Looking squarely ahead, brave joyous at the world,
The squads march to work.
All that matters to us now is Treblinka.
It is our destiny.
That's why we've become Treblinkas,
In no time at all.
We know only obedience and duty
We want to serve
To go on serving until little luck ends it all. Hurrah!

Susan Silas then imagined people stepping into the gas chamber with that song stuck in their heads. Her parents had endured the war in Eastern Europe, with her father being in a labour camp and her mother in a Jewish ghetto.

At the time when I witnessed the deprivations of the wandering children in 1948/9, I had met the airman who eventually became my husband and we watched these children with horror. Their numbers grew as they were joined by other similar groups, which now meant that there were those as young as three or four years of age and the oldest was probably 14. Many of our personnel gave them oranges and bread and even the occasional bar of chocolate. Jack and I took a great interest in Kurt, who was about

10 years old. He did not know when he was born or his actual age. For the year that we were in Bad Eilsen, we gave him clothes, often too large for him and boots and food. Then came the time when he came to the camp no more. The group had quite suddenly moved off. I have wondered so many times since then, what happened to them and did they get to have a happy life.

So what were my first impressions? At first, I felt I was in an alien world that seemed to have no connection with my life at home, in a seaside resort with traffic and shops and theatres and museums and above all, my parents and my own room. The war was over and though we had rationing still, we still in the main, ate familiar food, went to school, college or jobs and saw a future.

Now I was in a place with trees, many trees. It became very cold and there was snow that permeated and froze the body, until thought disappeared. The language was unfamiliar and what we saw of the populace seemed to be a uniform greyness, with few smiles, as they also struggled with the unfamiliarity of this situation that had encompassed Germany, so soon after the disastrous war. It took me some time to understand the job that I was doing, especially the reasons why it was so important. I did learn and I did accept the differences and in many ways I grew very fond of the area and the trees and the snow. More than that, I grew up and learned that Brighton and the south coast, indeed the UK, were not the only places in the world, also that other people had opinions and rights and love and hate and emotions, just as we had. I realised the futility of war and that in all these conflicts there are no winners. We all lose something important.

Chapter 3 – Life at the Camp

At first our environs were alien to us, a different country, a different language that we heard around us, even a different climate. We did have the security of a routine that we understood. We adhered to a Service routine, so made sure our uniform was always correct, that we saluted an officer when we met , we ate our meals at ordained times and partook of our meals in a canteen that looked uncannily like all the canteens that we had seen in our previous service life. We carried our 'irons' (cutlery) with us to meals, we collected our laundry each week, a sheet, a pillow case and a towel.

Jack and I collected our laundry, thence to walk to the canteen, carrying our 'irons'.

We learned that we would be paid in BAFVs, British Air Forces Vouchers, which were notes or brown coins, that gave the impression that we were paying for our 'treats' in the Malcolm Club with nothing more substantial than cardboard! We had little or no access to Deutschmarks, which meant that our buying potential was very limited and mostly 'in-house'. Shopping in the German shops was not an option. We obeyed the rules, knowing that if we transgressed in any way, we could face a charge and would get a fit punishment. On the whole, the menu presented at meals was as near to UK food as possible but somehow never quite tasted the same. We had to report for duty at the appropriate time and our hours were very long. The aircraft that were flying the food, coal and so many other goods needed to sustain life in Berlin,were making that hazardous journey every three minutes, 24 hours each day. We at Headquarters therefore, worked similar hours and after several weeks of insufficient sleep, we desperately needed recuperation and the chance to regain our energy. Jack and I were lucky enough to have several of these breaks at the same time and piled with others, into the camp gharry, an uncomfortable vehicle with little light and inadequate seating.

However, to us it was a holiday and we savoured every moment. Our venue was a Hotel in a mountain village called Scharfoldendorf (Scharf), where we were entertained by a small orchestra, more often than not, out of tune with each other. To us however, it was high romance. The highlight of our visits was our attempts to learn the art of gliding. These aircraft looked extremely fragile and we took our lives into our hands when we squeezed into the cockpit, one of us at a time, as we were accompanied by a German tutor. In effect, we were pushed to the top of a cliff and toppled off into space, with the hope that there would be thermals, upward draughts of hot air that would take us into the blue.

Primitive was not the word for it but to us it was the epitome of living on the edge, in more senses than one. Surprisingly, as far as I know, there were no accidents and we survived our visits to Scharf, intact. Years later when my husband worked for BOAC, which predated British Airways, the airline ran its own gliding club at the former RAF base at Booker, still in operation as the Wycombe Air Park. There however, the gliders were taken up in a very civilised fashion by a 'proper' aircraft and unhooked when thermals were discovered. Both my husband and son learned the art of gliding at that time but it was not half as much fun or entertaining, as on that mountain in Germany. One other incident at Scharfoldendorf that has continued to affect me, was that during one of our climbing days in that region. I actually fell down a mountain. I slipped and found myself tumbling down finally to become caught in a ridge that stopped my fall. I was remarkably unharmed, save for a twisted knee. For a time it was almost a bonus, as I was 'excused marching' and in fact, never did have to attend any marching exercise, for the rest of my service days. However, on occasion, I still have a re-occurrence of a very uncomfortable knee, which I call my, 'When I fell down a mountain at Scharfoldendorf complaint'.

Me and the glider!

Jack and I had met soon after my arrival at the camp. I was still anxious to continue with my singing training and in order to practise, I was told that I could use a piano in the Bade Hotel. I was outside, when I heard the strains of a piano being played and made my way to a beautiful room, in which there was a grand piano and an airman, who was playing the 'Warsaw Concerto'. I asked him to leave the piano, as I wanted to practise my singing and he refused. The altercation became quite heated, eventually leading to him leaving the room. We met later on, as we worked in the same building and came to the conclusion that a partnership, both in music and in life, may well be a solution.

I did appreciate the forest around us after a while and it certainly was a beautiful area. The village itself was most attractive, with a large park and of course the stream. It was such a picturesque stretch of water, sadly marred by the smell of the hydrogen sulphide. We soon learned however, that it was this particular malodorous mud, taken from the stream, that produced the rheumatism relief upon which the Spa had built its fine reputation. The whole village changed character in the winter, when deep snow covered the houses, the roads and the trees. We felt the cold badly and were not really equipped to cope with these weather conditions. The villagers just took it in their stride and I used to marvel at the children going to school on skis and really enjoying the snow on the slopes and in the woods.

I had travelled by boat to Belgium and then entrained to Germany when I first was sent out to work on the Airlift. So, the first time I had ever been on a 'plane was when I was sent with two other girls to Lubeck, to obtain some information. The aircraft was a very old Dakota with no seats and the portholes were covered in brown paper stuck to the fuselage with sticky tape. The bucket type seats were low and uncomfortable and I was terrified from the time I embarked. The aircraft flew only at 3000 feet, which meant that one of the Blackpool funfair rides was as nothing to the swoops and dives made as we flew over trees and hedges. We were given a brown package tied with string, containing very thick sandwiches, the sight of which enhanced my feelings of sickness to such an extent, that I just laid down and felt the certainty that I would never get up again.

The 'plane of course did land and I did get up and stagger across the runway, hardly able to believe that I was still alive. My life since has been full of travel and I have flown to most countries in the world, perfectly safely and with enjoyment which was all very surprising, as on the journey to Lubeck, I had sworn that I would never put foot on an aircraft again.

A signal had been sent to Lubeck, prior to our visit to explain who we were and our required duties. Accommodation had been requested for us and we were looking forward to a meal and bed. However there was a complication. I still have the Signal that was sent as a permanent reminder of the whole experience, a copy of which is now embedded in the cover illustration of this book. My maiden name was Peachey and the Signal was worded as such:

'REQUEST PERMISSION LACW HARRISON ACW OWEN AND RPT AND PEACHEY MAKE DUTY VISIT AIR TRAFFIC CONTROL.'

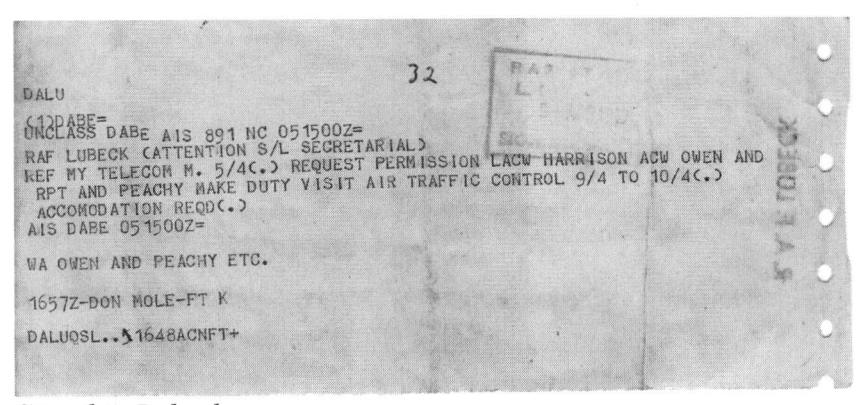

Signal to Lubeck

To those who received the signal it was assumed that 'Peachey' was a dog. I found the initial reception to my arrival somewhat disturbing, especially as the accommodation selected for me was not quite the billet and bed that I had expected!

Lubeck was on the border with the Russian sector, with the division marked by a stream. We were told that it was dangerous on the other side of the stream, as there could be trouble if we were caught. In fact it was intimated that we could even be shot. In the event, the nearest Soviet was some distance away but nevertheless, our action was extremely silly. Several of us jumped the stream with the stupidity of youth. We were told very firmly that our behaviour was foolish and against rules and were reminded of the consequences, had there been retribution. Many years forward in time, I re-visited Lubeck, which by that time had become a civil airport and I re-visited the stream, now no longer enemy territory but I realised, quite forcibly, that we had put ourselves in great danger.

We were sent home by train after we had completed our information collecting. Rickety and grubby though it was, I was grateful not to be hedge-hopping in a Dakota.

I was surprised when I was sent with five others, to Neuhaus in the American sector, to spend a few days with similarly aged German youths, who had been members of the Hitler Youth. The idea was to allow us to meet with them, have joint leisure activities and informal conversations, alongside the more formal talks, which then included the officers in charge. Our leaders were RAF Chaplains, Padre Milne, Padre Morley and Padre Sanders and I was led to believe that the Methodist church had an influence in this joint meeting of youngsters affected by the war, though from 'opposite' sides.

I have always assumed that my being sent to Neuhaus was an official RAF temporary posting, as part of my job and to widen my experience. Recently, I discovered a photograph showing a large group of RAF and WAAF personnel outside of a building, with the name, St.Rhad's, October 1947, in my handwriting. In the group are four officers, all are RAF Padres. After making enquiries, I have discovered that St. Rhad's (St. Rhadigund's) was and still is, a Christian Conference Centre on the Isle of Wight.

The present general manager, Mr Andrew Gardner has kindly sent me some information regarding the, 'Moral Leadership' courses, that were organised in the late forties and to which groups of we servicemen/women were sent. Although, I had hazy recollections of this event, after studying the photo, I recognised the padres. So where had I seen them before? Or since? I reviewed the material on the Neuhaus visit and was astonished to find that the padres in the photograph taken with the German Youth, were the same Padres who had been our mentors at St, Rhad's on the Isle of Wight, a year before. I can only assume now that the Padres had been sent to Germany to oversee similar courses, joining both the British and the German young people. They perhaps discovered my name at Bad Eilsen and remembered my previous visit with them and felt that I may be useful.

A further coincidence has occurred, in that a German civilian, who worked in my building at Bad Eilsen, Gunther Herzog and who still lives in Buckeburg , has kindly send me much material about his time during the war and also his life during the Airlift. He also was sent, as a civilian youngster to Neuhaus, to a 'Moral Leadership' course. He was not there at the same time as myself but we appear to have felt similarly, that In effect, we were junior ambassadors. More of his life is chronicled later in this book.

At the time, I felt very keenly the importance of discovering why the German teenagers had joined the Nazi Youth, including learning of the sorts of activities that they had undertaken and finally, how they felt about it all, in retrospect. I was only twelve when the war began and but even so, recognised the change of our life style, even to the carrying of gas masks. The air raids often meant that places we had always known in Brighton which had been bombed and destroyed, then left us with a feeling that we had lost our freedom alongside the buildings.

We had been brainwashed by newspapers and the 'wireless', into thinking that all German Nationals were 'Nazis'. Few of we teenagers knew what Nazism was but we believed that 'they' were violent and dangerous and were anxious to invade the world. They wore uniforms which supported a special symbol and were saluting with a forward movement of the arm at every occasion. My mother was blown across the road in a bomb blast and that coloured my sister's and my viewpoint, as to the nature of our enemy. For years after the war, playground games were make-believe fights between the British and the Germans. The British was the favourite 'gang' and always won.

Therefore only a few years later, I found myself with some surprise, staying for a while, with young Germans of my age group. It was quite a shock when their chief interest seemed to be pop music, girls/boys, dancing and having 'fun'. I have no doubt that the teenagers in besieged Berlin were materially very poor in clothes, books and of course food and fuel. Tom and Elfriede and Wulf and the others I met in Neuhaus, were of course living outside Berlin, often in rural areas and therefore better fed and clothed and more to the point, had more freedom than their peers in Berlin. They still lived with shortages however, and I remember drinking coffee at Neuhaus that was largely wood dust. However, the Americans, in whose zone we were, had their PBX, where chocolate was available to them and we were happy recipients every so often. All we youngsters went for long walks over the hills and talked much between ourselves, or sometimes led by the officers and leaders.

Group picture at Neuhaus

From left to right
Top Row- *Herbert, Susan, Gizela, Dieter, Mae, Brian.*
Middle Row -*Vernon,Tom, Wulf, Margarita, Franz, Hans, Harold.*
Bottom Row- *Myself, Elfriede, Padre Sanders, Padre Morley, Padre Milne, Padre Douglas, Hildegarde, Myrtle.*

When I returned to the UK after my demobilisation, Tom and Elfriede and I (then always known as 'Jo'), wrote letters to each other for a few months until it sadly petered out, as happens with most of distance correspondence. I have one letter from each of them in my possession even now. The surprise at the time, was that both were written in English. Sadly my German never really got beyond, 'Guten Morgen'. 'Danke', 'Bitteschon', 'Wie spat it es?' and 'Alles Gut'.

Elfriede wrote from Kellberg:

Many thanks for your letter, I received it on 5th January .(1949) Every day, I wanted to write some words to you, and every time I had other work. I had a fine Christmas. I got from my parents books and other trifles. I hope you had a Happy New Year. On New Year's Eve I visited Margarete (another member of our group . She lives in Eschershausen, not far from me. There I was five days and we had very fine hours. On 7th January our school begun again. Our holidays were very short for ourself, 3 weeks.

Many thanks for Myrtle's salutations (Myrtle was a WAAF). Before Christmas I wrote to her to England but I do not know if she got it. Dear Jo (my nickname at the time), you spell the word not quite correctly, so ist (this) is right, 'ist bin mude' (I am tired).

You wrote;- 'perhaps I will see you again one day'.

It would be very fine, it would be very fine but now, at this moment, I do not know how it could be. But we'll hope the best.

Best wishes to you and Myrtle. Yours truly. Elfriede'

Her punctuation and spelling was shaky but still miraculous compared to my understanding of German, both spoken and written. I am sure she stayed with safe subjects and words that were within her limits of the English language. Nevertheless, it was the letter of a 19 year old girl, apparently living the same sort of life as myself. The next letter was sent by Tom, an extrovert, full of life and always cheerful. One could say, a 'ladies man', as a useful description of this young teenager.

Dear Jo, Dear Myrtle, Lubeck Febr. 21

Yeah, I know I'm a bad boy, not having answered your letter as promptly as you answered mine and it's been quite some time since your very delightful letter arrived. But I was sure glad to hear from you and to know that everything was going fine. The trouble was that we had our final school examinations lasting till last week and so I couldn't possibly spare a minute to drop you a few lines. But now, lucky enough, we are out of school.

At the end of January we had the first part of our exams, German Composition, Englisch Composition, Latin translation, Mathematics and so forth. I fixed the Englisch (with 'c' erased this time) and Mathematics works okay but my German composition was no good at all. And then last week, some big-shot came to put school and after having asked all kinds of silly questions for another five hours, he told us that we had all past the final school examination okay. We were mighty glad, I tell you so!!!

Oh boy, it's a grand feeling to be out of school and to be rid of all kinds of school work. Nest week we are going to have our final school – dance and final celebrations. First I am going to take it easy for while and then I'll start working at the factory here in Lubeck to become an engineer. In about half a year I will start over to Hannover for final studies. Right now I am having a grand time together with Wulf, sleeping till late in the morning, doing a little bit of sports, listening to the radio or popping to the movies. Tonight we are gonna see Danny Kay in the, 'secret life of Mr. Something'. It is supposed to be a mighty good picture.

Well, that's about myself right now. I think you heard that Duggie (Padre Louis) was transferred to Buckeburg. Have you ever seen him again? I think he was a little bit too revolutionary for certain people over here. So now it became pretty lonely over here. But if you should ever come to Lubeck don't forget to drop in and say hello. In summer there are good opportunities to go swimming or we could have a game of lawn tennis, were I will certainly beat you. The only trouble is, that I haven't got the balls I need so I asked Vern whether he could send me them. Have you had any news from him lately? I've got a long letter from him and have just answered it. I often remember that a fine week we spent up in there in Neuhaus. We had quite some fun strolling around the mountains are playing records (remember?) hadn't we?

Now you gals, I think that's the rural vote this time, say hello to Jack and Jimmy were you? Well keep smiling and drop me a few lines in the future that you? Love from Tom. Wulf says hello too.

Tom had obviously been influenced by his association with the Americans stationed in his area who had coloured his version of the English language. As with Elfriede, his letter reflected the sorts of subjects that would have been covered by almost any teenager. In our conversations with our mentors at Neuhaus, he had seemingly noticed that there were differences of opinion about the events being played out at that time in Germany, among the British personnel, though he did not expand on these opinions in letters to me.

I did elicit some information from these youngsters with whom I spent that valuable time. From their parents they had learned of Hitler's belief that the Hitler Youth was part of his long-time plan for his Empire and that the future of Nazi Germany was its children. In the early 1920s, the Nazi party had established a youth movement with their leader being Kurt Gruber, its aim being the attraction of young men to be trained to become members of the SA (Stormtroopers).

On 4 July 1926, the movement was given a new name, the Hitler Youth, (Hitler Jugend.) These boys wore uniforms, attended meetings and took part in rallies, where they were brainwashed with Nazi views, as Hitler believed it was vital that the next generation were loyal to Nazi views to ensure the future strength of the third Reich. By 1930 there were 25,000 members. When the Nazis came to full power in 1933, other youth groups in the country were incorporated into the movement, which meant that by the end of 1933, there were 2 million youngsters being indoctrinated. In fact by 1936, to be a member of the Hitler Youth became compulsory for all those over 10 years old, with very few excuses allowed for non-membership, so that, by the beginning of the war in 1939, there were 8 million members.

Girls and boys were in separate branches, with the girls being trained to become good housewives and ultimately assume the role of the perfect German mother. Both boys and girls were trained in the Nazi views on a racial purity and anti-Semitism. The whole of the Hitler Youth Movement was masterminded by Balder von Shirach and to us, the whole organisation was the personification of German discipline. Actually, I have read recently that this picture was not quite accurate, as the constant attendance at the meetings usually every evening and weekends, devalued their school attendance to the point that these young people were too tired to concentrate on their lessons. In fact, during 1938, the attendances at the Hitler Youth meetings became very poor, which was one of the reasons why the rules were tightened considerably and attendance was made compulsory. There were many whose outlook was coloured for the rest of their lives. Perhaps Tom and Elfriede were the lucky ones.

There was certainly no compulsion for us but we were encouraged to visit and pursue one of the many subjects that were on offer in the Education Centre in Buckeburg, our nearest small town. We felt at that time, that one of the objects of this venture was to keep us occupied and trouble-free in what little spare time we were allowed from our duties. There were added incentives, in that to get to Buckeburg, we had to travel in the little local train, the 'Kleinbahn', which we soon christened, 'The Puffing Billy'. For a few brief moments away from the stress of the daily workload, we felt that we were off on a day trip to the seaside, or to the zoo.

In addition, we were able to visit the Malcolm Club where unusually at that time, white bread rolls were available and we made full use of that luxury. Jack and I found that music was one of the subjects on offer to us and gladly took advantage of the opportunity. We were more than fortunate to be taught by Herr Friedrich Seufert, who had been a professor of music at Frankfurt University. He was bombed out of his home and lost his wife and children in the blast and in consequence, he found that his position at the University was untenable. Later, the University itself sustained considerable damage.

He accepted the job at the Buckeburg Education Centre, in order to earn a living. I am sure that the fact that I am still able to sing usefully in a choir, even in my eighth decade, is mainly based on that year's excellent tuition. I felt embarrassed for him when we bought him rolls and buns when we had our breaks, as it became obvious to us that he had no food with him, nor the wherewithal to buy any refreshments. He gave one or two excellent concerts. I have one of his programmes still in my possession. When I returned to the UK, I wrote to Herr Seufert and in his reply, he thanked me for the letter and the photograph that I had enclosed, 'which will be a lasting memory for me.'

Herr Friedrich Seufert, Music Professor, at the Education Centre Buckeburg

He talked about his work in Buckeburg, that he was still teaching music there and was giving recitals every month. He was very glad to tell me that he had been playing on Radio Frankfurt and that he hoped to return to Frankfurt where he had already had discussions with government officials to see if he could return to the Academy as a Professor. Sadly this would not be possible for some time as many bomb-damaged buildings had to be rebuilt and this work could take at least a year.

He described life in Germany and explained that it had become much easier to get foodstuffs. The shops were beginning to be filled with wonderful things but sadly the people themselves did not have enough money to buy them, in fact even to buy the things that they really needed. Clothes in particular were still very expensive. Food rationing had been lifted and everything was now freely on sale. He gave the example of one egg being 50 to 60 pfennig at Christmas time but now, in March, the price was down to 17 to 18 pfennig. Meat and sausage was somewhat cheaper but still too expensive for most people. He went on to say that in West Germany, there were over 2 million unemployed and in his opinion, that was a very bad state for the country to be in but the government had promised an improvement.

He concluded by sending us good wishes for our marriage and wished us all the best of the future. He said he was certain that our children would be very musical and he wished that he could teach them music in the future. We had no correspondence after that letter, which was a great pity, particularly as both our children are musical, as are my grandchildren and their families.

At the same time as I was at the camp at Bad Eilsen, there was a young girl, Ingrid, 18 years old, who lived in a small village, near to the town of Spandau, which became part of the eastern sector. As she said to me when we met years later in the UK, 'then the Russians came and that is a big story on its own.'

It was obvious that she had very unpleasant memories of the Soviet invasion. She did say that it was not safe for young girls until the Russians eventually left.

'It was a very bad time, living on the Russian side. I would not like to write the whole story of what I know'. She did tell me that she and her family did not get much food, so her father decided to keep sheep, which fed on grass in their rather large garden. 'When it was the airlift, I used to go down to where the sheep were and lie flat on my back in the grass and look up at the big 'planes going over. They were so big and so low down and I think this is because if there had been any higher, then the Russians would have shot them down. We didn't get any of the food and other things that the planes were bringing but my father used to bring home chocolate that workers had got hold of and given him. That is because he worked in the western sector and came home every night. He was allowed to go from one sector to the other for work. People who are living on the Russian side were allowed to cross over but that was until the wall went up and that happened overnight'.

In fact later, when the Berlin Wall was erected, Ingrid's father was trapped in the western sector. Her mother did manage to visit him once but he could not return home with her, he had to stay in West Berlin. She tells of the Russians entering houses and taking anything that they fancied, they even took her mother's clothes out of her wardrobe at one point. She told me the story of how some friends of theirs had managed to get through the Wall with a horse and cart and with sacking round the horse's hoofs, to prevent the noise. They took as much from the house as they could and then returned to the West, where their treasures were stored until the wall eventually came down.

When Ingrid was 21, she married a soldier who had been serving in the British Army in Germany during the Airlift and when I met her, she was living in East Sussex.

We were not encouraged to fraternise, so although we worked with German civilians, it was difficult to find out how they were living their lives on a day-to-day basis, even though in theory, they were free to live their ordinary routines at home and work. The local people in the Bad Eilsen area were not under siege as were the Berliners but they did suffer from shortages and were deeply distressed and concerned about the pressure that their country was under and full of concern as to the future.

We were even less knowledgeable about the citizens in other parts of Germany, including those who lived in the American zone, as each other zones were very influenced by those in charge, whether French, American, British or of course Russian. I did have the good fortune to visit the American zone, which was a great adventure to be able to travel the countryside and I did notice that the PBX canteen was able to supply luxuries, such as scented soap, chocolate and silk stockings which of course were articles which we rarely, if ever, saw. At the same time, the sweets that were available at the American barracks were also used to give the Berlin children a very welcome treat.

In July 1948, an American pilot, Gail Halvorsen, as a single man, came to Frankfurt as a replacement for a married man with a family. He had been on operations for several days when on a free day, he flew as a passenger to Berlin so as to see the situation in that city, for himself. He was walking inside the perimeter fence of the airfield to take some photographs of the aircraft as they landed, when he saw a group of children. They were clean though poorly dressed and he was concerned by their passive behaviour, with none of the begging that he had seen in other countries. We must remember that, at the time, the 1939-45 war was only three years in the past and relationships between the German people and the Allies was sensitive and insecure.

Over time, the children started to trust Halvorsen and no longer viewed the uniform of the 'enemy' as a dread symbol of wartime terror. One day, as they were at the fence and he was worrying about their future, he realised that he had nothing to offer them and in his pocket he found two pieces of chewing gum, both of which he broke into halves. He gave them to the children who had spoken to him, using the English that they had learned at school and was shocked to see how treasured this gum was to them as even the paper wrappers were folded and kept. Halvorsen then devised a way of dropping sweets and gum to them from the aircraft, as they flew over Berlin. He told the children to look for the 'plane that wiggled it wings as it flew overhead, then they would know that it was him. The only way to ensure that the sweets would land was to make 'parachutes' from large handkerchiefs. By borrowing handkerchiefs and any other available cloth and by accepting chocolate and gum from the other pilots, Halvorsen carried on his mission to give these children some joy, amidst the sorrows of the recent war and now living in a besieged city. As time went by, more and more of the pilots joined him in dropping the 'parachutes', all over Berlin and we remember them as the 'Candy Bombers'.

Many years later, a German lady called Johanna Hoppe was recalling her life during the Airlift in Berlin. Her mother had been very ill and she was put into a Protestant childrens' home near General Clay's Barracks. In a letter to all veterans much later in her life, she said that she had been well looked after in the children's home, meaning that they had been kind to the children. She said that the nearby barracks had supported the children and had given them tree decorations at Christmas and Easter, made out of fondant. She spoke of the handkerchief parachutes and the pleasure they had given at a time when there was very little joy.

In gratitude, in 2005-2007, Johanna decided to thank all the veterans who helped the 'Berliners' by giving handkerchiefs as a present. She designed all the handkerchiefs herself and this included the lettering and painting. She created 135 different weaves, colours and patterns. I have been privileged to receive a handkerchief – mine is numbered 302 and with the handkerchief was a letter, from which I gathered the above information about the Childrens' Home. My handkerchief has flowers and trees, swans, little parachutes with a box of candy and is inscribed, 'Unforgotten', 'Liberty and Friendship', 'Thank you for the Berlin Airlift 1948-1949', 'One little piece of Berliner-soul'.

I cherish my handkerchief and it is indicative of the gratitude that is still shown to us by the Berliners, for the year of 1948, when the Allies sustained the city through the Russian Blockade.

The story of Colonel Halvorsen did not end his kindness to children after the Airlift. Then retired, he visited Albania in 1999 to deliver school supplies, sweets and toys to the Kosovar Albanian refugee children, who were escaping from the then Serb oppression. He flew in a C-130 transport 'plane to Tirano to visit Camp Hope. The USA-built camp was opened to give shelter 20,000 refugees, who were the victims of the civil strife in Yugoslavia. Much has happened in that area since that time but he is still remembered by those who had been so excited to have received, 'candy and gum'. *(from News Service – US Air Forces in Europe – 15.12.02)*

Baerbel Simon, a great friend of the British Berlin Airlift Association, contacted me recently, to give me details of her life in Berlin during the Airlift. She was born in 1947 and lived close to Templehof, in the American sector. Her mother was a nurse in one of the West Berlin hospitals and her grandfather owned a small factory, where he made woodwind instruments, clarinets and bassoons. The Americans took their instruments to him for any repairs and they paid him with food and any other goods which were available to them. Her aunt lived in the French sector where she used her skills as a dressmaker to make clothes for the ladies.

Barbels's uncle helped to build Tegel Airport, also in the French Sector. She was told stories of the Second World War by her grandmother and she herself can remember the Airlift, especially of the low-flying aircraft and the loud roar of the engines. She was still very young and the noise and the shadows cast on the ground by the 'planes were very frightening to her. Her grandmother had consoled her,

'Listen girl, they are good people. They're bringing us food, coal and medicine, to survive'.

Barbel contracted whooping cough at the beginning of 1949, which was very dangerous as she, like all the children, were not only young but under weight and undernourished. However, the doctor prescribed an antibiotic, which became available to her through the medical supplies dropped by the 'planes. Baerbel still honours the Airlift Veterans and is the Director of the Cold War Museum. We are all getting old now, even those young children in Berlin in 1948 but she wrote that,

'In our hearts the young Airlift heroes, flyers and ground crews, will live forever. One thank-you cannot be enough. Time flies and it is time to inform and to teach the young, with the plea to carry on this work.'

She is right, we need somehow, to educate the young to realise that in all wars and confrontations, there are no winners. One of the songs we sing in our choir here in Cornwall, exhorts us to, 'Live our lives in Peace and Harmony.'

At least Baerbel can say now, that she has had good relationships with the Western allies all of her life and that she had grandparents who set her on the right path in the past and pointed her towards the future. Now she can say proudly, 'Ich bin ein Berliner' (Proud to be a Berliner).

Baerbel's husband Horst, was born in 1943 close to the now, 'Platz der Luftbruecke'. Horst's home had been bombed during the war, as were his neighbours but in 1945 the rubble was removed and re-building began. He remembers a happy childhood then. There was no rationing and they 'managed, even though there was not a great deal of money for food and coal.'

The West Berliners had been following the political development of their city and realised that the goal of the Soviets, was to take over West Berlin. He remembers the closure of all the routes into Berlin and realised that soon they were unable to buy fresh groceries and other staples. Horst also lived near to Templehof and remembers the roar of the aircraft. The 'planes flew low to remain undetected by the Soviets. He remembers the people being given information on the radio (RIAS – Radio in the American Sector) and looking at advertising pillars, showing the places where they could use their food stamps and pick up the food that was being dropped onto the city. Horst said that,

'From then on I ate a lot of dried potatoes and vegetables, dried milk powder, egg powder and much more as well.'

Meat came in cans, oil and margarine were heavily rationed. Once each week, they had a treat of some freshly baked bread. If they took more than one slice of this delicious food, then they would have to have one less the next day.

Horst considered himself very lucky when the Blockade was over as he did not have to eat dried potatoes and vegetables any longer. He still has what he calls a 'Blockade phobia', as even today, he still keeps a four-week supply of groceries such as pasta and canned vegetables, in his storage – just in case!

I have included these stories here as during the time that these children were living in these adverse conditions, I was at Bad Eilsen. I am not sure that we, as youths, appreciated the difficulties being endured. We were keeping the city alive we believed, without really realising the political, economic, psychological and physical health despondency that has never quite left the Berliners, even today.

Nevertheless, we did work tremendously hard and just once during the year, I was sent for a weekend of rest and recuperation, back to the UK and home.

I flew into Northolt, a civil airfield and thence by train to Victoria Station, to enable me to get a further train to Brighton. In Bad Eilsen, we had been issued with trousers and yellow leather gauntlet gloves, mainly because of the intense cold once the winter had descended upon us.

I wore the trousers and the gloves on the journey back, as they had become a usual part of my uniform and was startled to find two burly SP's (Air Force Police) descend upon me at Victoria and they held my arms, so that I felt imprisoned and very frightened. They asked me my name and,

'Why was I on Victoria Station and wearing improper dress?'

I told them that I was on leave from Germany and on the way home to Brighton and that I was wearing the correct uniform as was the normal in Germany. They simply did not believe me, having never seen the yellow gauntlet gloves and indeed WAAF personnel in trousers, unless they were actually engaged upon a job for which they were suited, e.g., a driver. I was taken to a room and questioned for a very long time. They must have telephoned a higher authority, as eventually I was allowed to continue travelling, with the stricture that I take off the gloves there and then and change into my uniform skirt, which was in my rucksack. I suppose I was most surprised that they were unaware of different modes of dress dependent on where one was stationed. They hated the yellow gloves and I suppose, looking back, they were rather conspicuous!

We were allowed to travel the short distance to Buckeburg on the 'Puffing Billy' for suitable recreation. Occasionally we went to the cinema in Buckeburg and the day came when Jack and I walked along the street to the cinema, holding hands. There were a group of us and cheerfully made our way to our 'treat', when two hefty SPs came up to us and actually put their hands on my shoulders. I was alarmed and thoroughly mystified until we were told very sharply that holding hands whilst in uniform was an offence.

'You also have the top button of your great coat open', they said, in steely tones.

I was petrified and felt that somehow unknowingly, I had effected a crime that would harm my country. I was put on a charge ('a fizzer') but was allowed to continue to the cinema where we watched, 'The Way to the Stars', containing the poem 'Johnny in The Clouds', or sometimes just, 'For Johnny', which is still one of my favourites.

> Do not despair
> For Johnny head-in-air
> He sleeps as sound
> As Johnny underground
>
> Fetch out no shroud
> For Johnny-in-the-cloud
> And keep your tears
> For him in after years.

Better by far
For Johnny the bright star
To keep your head
And see his children fed
(John Pudney, Shepheard-Walwyn, pub.)

'The Way to the Stars', was a British War drama set in 1945 and the title was taken from the Latin motto of the RAF, Per Ardua Ad Astra, which I have always translated as, 'Through Difficulties to the Stars'. The alternative American title to the film was, 'Johnny in the Clouds' and came from the poem, which was recited in the film as a touching tribute to a dead American airman. I cried through the performance, both at the film and the heartache it portrayed and to a degree, my own mortal fear of the oncoming charge – standing before the office confessing my crime of unfastening my top button. In the event, the officers were very kind and did no more that warn me not to hold hands in the street and to be properly dressed at all times.

One of my tasks was to send messages, often world-wide, as directed by my Controller. On one occasion, I sent the news winging through the atmosphere, that Gatow Zoo had been blown up and was now destroyed. This must have been an horrific shock to the world at large. The zoo and its environs, plus all the animals therein, would have been seen as a disaster. Later that day, I received a signal from my commanding officer which informed me that indeed, it was only a flak tower that had been involved. That was all the remonstration that I received much to my relief, though my error did provoke much mirth amongst my fellow workers. As already reported, I was told several years later the fact there was great importance attached to the flak tower, so that did make me feel a little better.

I also discovered later that from the 10th December, 1940, as a result of a personal order from Hitler, the construction began of 'Flaktume', which were anti- aircraft towers, designed to protect the city from bombing. The first two Towers were built in the

Tiergarten, where the zoo is situated and another in the Friedrichshain, with the third in the Humboldthain Park, all before 1942. The flak bunkers could be seen soaring over the locality. Each tower contained anti-aircraft cannons, were accepted as completely bombproof and there was also a space of 15,000 civilians. So they were very large edifices. After the war, the Berlin flak towers were blown up as military structures, by the French.

I understand that the Humboldthain Flak Tower still remains as a ruin and the Berlin Underworlds Association has been able to make this site accessible to the public. Apparently 1.5 million cubic metres of rubble were piled on top of the remains to create a 'mountain of debris'. At the time, I felt embarrassed because I had mistaken the flak tower in the Tiergarten for the whole zoo but learning the facts in after years, I began to realise that though I was not entirely accurate, the operation was a great deal larger and of more importance than I had first believed.

As part of my job I became interested in the loads that were carried by the aircraft flying to Berlin. Our communications with the aircraft were largely to do with the cargo, along with types of departure and arrival and routes to fly. Part of these rag bags of remembrances, concerns the contents of the thousandth load.

The main load was probably coal and also, there was a consignment of contraceptives. This particular flight was feted all over the world as being a high point in the vital operation of the airlift, simply because it was the thousandth. Few people would have known the contents. Being in the 'know', I felt slightly embarrassed but in those days it was rather a dark subject, certainly not a discussion point in my home. Years later, when I was a Head of a school in Surrey, I used to have regular and official visits from the Clerk of Works from my local Education Authority. I used to offer him a cup of tea and during our chat, I discovered that he had been in the RAF. I told him of my involvement and we were mutually surprised that we had both served in Germany. I told him the story of the thousandth load and he laughed uproariously. He was actually the Observer of the aircraft. After that, whenever I needed a window mending, or the boys loos unblocking, usually difficult to achieve quickly, I would telephone him and say, 'Remember the thousandth load', and workmen would be at the school within hours!!

Every so often, we went to Hameln (Hamelin) in organised parties and found it to be an attractive town with obvious signs of the 'Pied Piper' and effigies of the mice, on buildings in all the streets. The poem, by Robert Browning, which had been part of my childhood, became a regular offering when I later became a teacher, being particularly impressive, as I could inform my pupils that I had visited the town. In Hamelin, the legend tells of a Piper dressed in two colours (Pied), who charmed the children from their homes by his magical piping and led them away to a far off mountain, where they disappeared for ever. I was told that the origin of the story went back to the Black Plague in Europe in the 14th century, when many of the local children died, taken away by this dreadful disease, represented by the Piper. Perhaps there are other reasons why the town was bereft of children for many years but this one does seem plausible. In 1348, there were 500,000 victims in Europe. The same Plague attacked London in 1665, with equally disastrous results.

Once or twice we were taken to Hannover (Hanover) to visit the Speedway Racing. The track was created out of cinders and my chief memory is a black choking dust and we onlookers spending weeks trying to get the particles out of our uniforms We also visited the opera in Hannover, which was a treat for me and also gave us an insight into the determination of the German people to effect some normality.

Life on the Camp was totally alien when I first arrived but has remained with me as one of the most valuable years of my life. Looking back and realising the expected and pedestrian life that I may have had if I had not been in the RAF and in particular my small involvement in the Berlin Airlift, I count my days in Bad Eilsen as enlightening, a source of my interest in psychology and people's behaviours, history in all of its facets and of course music and all that has meant to me and the family over the years.

Chapter 4 - And Afterwards

In another Dakota, I flew to RAF Halton on 25th May, 1949 for my demobilisation. 'Demob' was a very odd experience and we had to line up in the stock room and hand over our uniform. I have often wondered how personnel were able to retain their uniforms, or at least the caps. It certainly was not a possibility for me. I had worn this clothing for two years with few new additions and I felt suddenly bereft, as if part of me was being taken from me. I felt odd in my 'civvies' and even odder when I was given my discharge papers and then suddenly, I was 'out'. We all went off in different directions and I found myself alone, on a Brighton train.

On the train I looked at my 'Statement of Service and Certificate of Discharge'. I was quite shocked and pleasantly surprised at their, 'Brief statement of any special aptitudes or qualities or any special types of employment for which recommended'.

'A keen and conscientious worker who can be relied on and trusted. She should do well in civilian life and is readily adaptable to changing conditions and is anxious to continue her studies'.

I also had a 'Very Good' character. Praise of any kind had not been forthcoming during my service. Perhaps there is a good reason for this omission and I have to agree that there were more important issues to be considered especially during the Airlift, which had so seriously affected the lives of thousands of people.

I married soon after. My husband obtained a position with BOAC (British Overseas Airways Corporation) and with a young daughter and even younger son, we moved into the London area. Heathrow Airport really was a 'heath' at that time and we watched it grow, both in size, buildings and numbers of passengers. We carried our own cases to the aircraft and with few people flying then, in the 1950s/1960s, the aircraft were more often than not, half empty and we travelled in comfort and received much attention from the stewardesses, in their immaculate navy blue and white uniforms. BOAC and BEA (British European Airways) later amalgamated and became British Airways, for which my husband worked for the remainder of his life.

When the children were somewhat older, I went to Teacher Training College and thus began my career in education. I became a Head Teacher, obtained a doctorate and focused a great deal of my energy on working within all aspects of dyslexia. I was also admitted as a Chartered Member of the British Psychological Society, so have been able to work as an advisor in many problem areas. I continued with this work after my retirement from school and have been a consultant, assessor and lecturer to this day. I have always written articles and even published a book on dyslexia and after my experiences with the British Berlin Airlift Association, it seemed a natural consequence to write a further book, this time recalling my memories of the Airlift itself, as that year was such an influence in my life.

Inevitably, I have written my recollections from the standpoint of being British and working within a British RAF-controlled camp. There was little opportunity to meet with our fellow Allies, as largely we kept to the boundaries of our own organisation. I learned about the involvement of the other nations as time went by and realised that there were others taking a significant role in the Blockade, the Americans of course, taking an immensely important role. Nevertheless, the exploits of the pilots of the US aircraft and the part played by General Lucius D. Clay, have tended to overshadow the extraordinary exploits of the British airmen and the enormous part that General Robertson, Air Commodore Rex Waite and politicians, such as Ernie Bevin, played in the preparations and delivery of the Berlin Airlift. John Tusa *(Seminar at the Royal Aeronautical Society - The Berlin Airlift 1948-1949)*, mentioned seeing the plaque to Lucius Clay at Templehof Airport , which nobody would deny to him. However, he was described as the 'architect' of the Airlift, which is somewhat of an overstatement.

Tusa also pointed out that there was a Clay Allee in Berlin but not a Robertson Allee and I noted too that there was not a Waite Allee.

(2014, Recently, I have been reliably informed that since that time, there is now a street in honour of Waite, 'Rex-Waite-Strasse')

In reality, both the UK and the USA and many other nations, made huge contributions. The US totalled more tonnage and had more 'planes and equipment but certainly the UK undertook difficult tasks, such as the 'dangerous' loads and 'wet' loads and also organised the difficult job of obtaining the private fliers. Between us, we kept Berlin alive for a year and that was no mean feat.

The year 1949 was a watershed, not just for Germany but for Europe as well. That year, decisions were made about the future of Germany. On May 23rd, eleven days after the lifting of the blockade in Berlin, the Federal Republic of Germany was created from the Western zones. NATO (North Atlantic Treaty Organisation) was formed on August 24th. America, Canada and many of the non-Communist European countries, promised that they would offer mutual assistance in case of foreign aggression. On September 23rd, President Truman announced that the Russians had successfully exploded their first atomic bomb blast and concluded that they were now on par with the West.

On October 5, 1949 the German Democratic Republic was formally created from the Soviet zone in Germany and for the time being, there was a balance of a sort, with the frontier between the two halves becoming the front line of the European Cold War.

In Ann and John Tusa's book. *'The Berlin Airlift'*, the penultimate page mentioned that, 'everyone had talked of Berlin, 'getting back to normal', once the blockade was over.

'It never did. The city's story from 1949 is one of painfully slow adjustments to the abnormal. Communications between the western sectors and the outside world remained vulnerable to Soviet interference.' The book then tells of the erection of the, 'obscene concrete scar of the wall which mutilated the city'.

The Berlin Wall (Berliner Mauer) was a very real and physical barrier between East and West Berlin and in effect, Germany itself, from August 13th 1961 until November 9th, 1989. In reality of course, Berlin was in the Soviet Zone and although zoned between Russia and the three Allies, was an island inside communist East Germany. It could be said that the wall was built in an underhand manner in the middle of the night and was intended to prevent East Germans escaping to the West. Any positive relationship between the Soviet Union and the Allies had disappeared and in effect, the building of the Berlin wall was a battle between democracy and communism.

Both sides of the wall were very different, especially in living conditions, where the stark blocks of faceless flats remain. I have seen them recently and though there have been window boxes added and other decorations, the grey impersonal basic structures still reflect the lifestyle that was the 'Eastern side'. The capitalistic society of the West produced a totally different and affluent life style, even to the style of architecture, the food and goods available and the general freedom of the people. They experienced an extremely quick economy growth and the one freedom that gave them superior advantages over the East, was the ability to freely travel world-wide. There was a vastly different situation for the East Germans who who did not have freedom in any facet of their lives and in addition had much valuable factory equipment taken from the zone by the Russians and sent to Russia.

Under the influence of the Soviet Union, East Germany became a communist society. The economy was poor and personal liberties were drastically curtailed. Up to the 1950s, there had been an exodus from the East to the West, with many being stopped on the way and forcibly restrained. However, large numbers did reach the West, often those who were young, and had a professional training and even a career to take with them. East Germany lost much of its labour force and also was unhappy with the decrease in population. The East lost 2.5 million of its citizens by 1961 and measures needed to be put in place to stop further leakage. With the support of the Soviets, attempts were made to take over West Berlin, even to the extent of threatening the United States with the use of nuclear weapons. Nevertheless, the Western Allies stood resolute in their refusal to support the East in their efforts to stop the movements of citizens from the East to the West. In desperation, East Germany decided to build the wall to prevent any crossing of the border.

There were many East Germans who did attempt to escape to the west, even by physically climbing over the wall which was a highly dangerous manoeuvre, with the dual risk of badly falling or being shot. Families had been split during the speedy building of the wall and in many cases, it was many years before relatives were able to meet again. The wall stretched for over a hundred miles. Its path was not just through the centre of Berlin but enclosed all of West Berlin, effectively cutting off West Berlin from the rest of Germany. In the beginning it was built of barbed wire with concrete posts, then quickly became more permanent by concrete posts, though still topped with barbed wire. Then in 1965, the basic concrete was replaced by a concrete wall with steel girders. Following this structure, there was a fourth 'edition', which consisted of 12 feet high, 4 feet wide concrete slabs with a smooth pipe running across the top of the wall to stop escapees from climbing over to get to the West. Lives were lost by those trying to get back to their homes, their families or simply attempting to leave the severity of the Communist East.

The despondent last paragraph of the Tusa book, was written during 1989, the last year of the overwhelming presence of the Wall. At that time they wrote,

'The presence of troops was to be a constant reminder of the past and present problems which has not been solved. The city, cut by a wall, makes palpable the division of Europe and the hostility between the two Power blocs and two sets of political and economic beliefs. The city can never be reconstituted until there is a German Treaty, a united country and a peaceful European settlement. How and when will Berlin become a city like any other?'

The next year the wall came down. I have returned to Berlin several times to view the remains of the wall which are a constant reminder of the conflict that divided the city.

Sadly I have always felt that the city is still divided, that the final solution has yet to be found. Both sides of the Brandenburg Gate still feel separated and there is a palpable difference between the East and West sides.

We celebrated the lifting of the Blockade as a victory. In fact, since that time, I myself have repeated the story of our helping Berlin to survive to schools and organisations, rather than allow that year to disappear from the consciousness of all those who have been born since and have no knowledge or awareness of the struggle then to keep a country together. Looking back from my much greater age and experience, I know that it was not an event under which we should put a line, as if it was a self-contained episode which had a beginning, a middle and a finite ending. History always 'merges' the lifelines and the airlift was certainly part of a great on-going story that is still seeking answers and decisions.

Certainly the Airlift could be said to have been the beginning of the Cold War and then we saw a divided city in a divided country split by a great dividing wall, between East and West Berlin. This artificial separation lasted from 13th August 1961 until 9th November, 1989, when the wall was taken down. The Federal Republic had given a good start economically to a broken country and then being without the need for an all-out war, prosperity did return to a more secure Germany. Yet visiting the city today, there is still a sense that the Brandenburg Gate did not totally join the two sides, that somehow there is a division still. There is still a sensitivity between Russia, Germany, the USA and the UK and sadly, world harmony is still in the distance.

The British Berlin Airlift Association – *a snapshot of the many visits to Germany since the Blockade*

In May, 1994, some 45 years after the cessation of the Airlift, the decision was taken to close down Gatow and three U.K. ex Airlift veterans, took part in the ceremony.

They then decided to form a British Berlin Airlift Association, there having been a similar American organisation for some years and later that year, ten veterans, along with ten Americans, were honoured to be invited by the Berlin Senate to ceremonies on September 6th- 8th, which marked the withdrawal of the Western Allies from Berlin.

Over the following years the Association grew, with several hundred members, both men and women from all ranks, trades and experiences, the only criterion being, that they had been engaged either directly or indirectly, on the Berlin Airlift.

The years following the inauguration of the Association contained many trips made by the members to well-known and often historic places of interest in the U.K. and crucially, visits to Germany. We revisited the airfields, which had become such an important part of our lives and also the museums which house the mementoes of those years.

The commemoration service at Templehof in Germany, each year on May 12th, the date of the end of the Airlift, has always been the most important, nostalgic and meaningful to me and I suspect to most of the other members. There is a splendid memorial in the, 'Platz der Luftbrucke', with three soaring columns representing the three corridors, looking as if they are flying into the air. Time and the ageing process has taken away the ability of many of the veterans to effect this yearly visit and I fear that the service this year, 2014, is probably the last. Hopefully, even with the closure of Templehof as an Airfield, the memorial will still be there to remind us of the marvel of the year of 1948/9 and also to remember those who died so bravely.

However, in the earlier days of the Association, there were large numbers of veterans from the UK, USA, Germany and representatives from other countries concerned with the Blockade, that met to watch the German airmen lay colourful wreaths onto the base of the memorial contributed by each of the countries concerned. Ambassadors of the countries, Mayors, Clergy, Senior Officers of the Armed Forces, have been present to listen to the band, watch the fly-past and to hear the address given by the Mayor of Berlin. The Gratitude Committee set up in Berlin to thank all those that helped in those difficult days, is still in operation after all these years and it hosts activities and visits for all those who still visit on that important date.

It is sad to note that in the UK, the British Veterans have been largely forgotten over the intervening years and not until very recently has any interest been shown by the media or the government in the Airlift and the parts that we played in the saving of Berlin. One can only speculate as to the course of history, had we Allies not intervened so successfully.

I appreciated the visits that we have made to Germany, especially with regard to my being able to visit places that I had only heard or read about, and to replace my often muddled perceptions with reality, in regard to the political background of the environs in which I had worked. One successful visit was to the Schloss Cecilien, where in 1945, the Potsdam conference had been held between America, Britain and USSR. Whilst in that area, Neuer Park, we had a fascinating hour at the Sans Souci Park to look at the palace of Friedrich the Great, (Friedrich 2nd). I found it interesting, in that Crown Prince Wilhelm Friedrich, grandson of Kaiser Bill (Wilhelm), had commissioned the building of the Schloss Cecilien in the 1920s, as one of the buildings in the Neuer Park, where his great, great grandfather had built the great complex that is Sans Souci and still a landmark of huge architectural value to the people of Potsdam and Berlin.

Frederick 2nd (Friedrich), had been happier there, than living in Berlin. His wife, seemingly was a 'convenience' bride, as it was important for him to be married and have a suitable wife. He appeared to enjoy male company in preference to his poor spouse. The kitchen was outside the palace in a separate block, as the Emperor did not like the preparation of food to be effected in the building in which he was domiciled. Apparently, there were always problems with keeping the food hot in its transportation between buildings. Other palaces were added over the years and now there are seven palaces over an area of 740 acres and it is purported to be the largest and most beautiful of palace complexes, in all of Europe.

Friedrich 1st, his father, had been a powerful Emperor who turned his court into a near-military garrison. He was called the 'soldier king'. He was determined to enlarge the Prussian army and was responsible for forming a regiment of seven-foot tall guardsmen. Strangely, he advocated the notion of 'peace' and he rarely risked his regiments on the field of battle. He was not happy that his son, should become Friedrich 2nd, as he had shown an artistic, musical and philosophical interest and would often be beaten and humiliated by his father. Friedrich 2nd, 'ran away' with his friend Hans Herman von Katte but was eventually arrested and imprisoned by his Father. Hans Katte was beheaded for treason. Friedrich 2nd was freed from prison in order to marry Elizabeth Christine of Brunswick, a niece of the Hapsburg Emperor and he was therefore, just a political pawn.

Friedrich senior died and Friedrich 2nd, quickly disbanded his father's regiment of seven-foot soldiers. He also became quite ruthless in his policy of territorial expansion. He admired and met Bach and Voltaire, so was indeed a very complicated character. He died after catching a cold whilst reviewing his troops in a rainstorm. Another of the interesting items that I discovered during our visit, was that up until that time, Emperors had been Emperors *in* Prussia but when he died, he left a legacy of being Emperor *of* Prussia. He was buried at Sans Souci in 1919, long after his death.

Exploring my interest in the 'links' between countries, which usually entailed changes in boundaries, the subject of Prussia became very apt. Prussia was the name of an area in Northern Europe, though was part of Germany for a while and also included areas in Poland. It has been described as, ' The land of the Baltic Prussians' and the lands of the Teutonic knights (12th century soldiers who fought for their religious beliefs), though the label of, 'the largest area of the German Empire, the Weimar Republic and the Centre of Nazi Germany from 1939/1945, has been the most recent significant identity. Before 1934, these regions were also in Prussia,

West Prussia and East Prussia, which are now in Poland and Russia.
    Pomerania
    Silesia
    Brandenburg
    Lusatia
    Kingdom of Hanover
    Schleswig-Holstein
    Westphalia
    Parts of Hesse
    The Rhineland
Some small areas in the south, e.g Wurttemberg-Hollenzollern, the home of the leaders of Prussia.

    The Nazis dropped the name Prussia in 1934 and the allies abolished the state of Prussia and divided the land between the new German States.
    One of our visits (2000) was poignant and very pertinent to our party. We had set off from Lubeck for Berlin via Schonberg, so that we could lay a wreath in the Herrburg cemetery, which resembled a huge garden, beautifully kept and alive with flowers. The memorial was to the Dakota KN491, which crashed there. We had three survivors of the crash with us, including the pilot, which made our ceremony very moving. We also visited the hospital where, all those years ago, the pilot was treated, along with the other

survivors and our Chairman presented the hospital with an excellent framed print of a Spitfire. We were joined there by Wolfgang Huschke, who wrote, 'The Candy Bombers', a reference to the 'parachutes' of sweets that American air crews had dropped upon the children of Berlin. Over coffee, I told him the story of my sending the wrong message to the world, with reference to the 'blowing up' of the Berlin Zoo, which in fact turned out to be 'only' a flak tower. Wolfgang became quite agitated and explained that much political intrigue had taken place in the tower and that the action of destroying it, was of a really serious nature.

'Checkpoint Charlie', had been discussed many times and obviously had been of great a importance, though was just a name to me. Berlin, the blockade and all those people under siege, subsumed our lives, took all our concentration and waking hours, yet for most of us in stations outside of the city, Checkpoint Charlie and indeed Berlin itself, remained names on a page or a signaller's description. It was therefore of enormous interest when I finally visited the place where, after the building of the Wall, Checkpoint Charlie had served as a crossing point for the diplomats, embassy members, the allied forces and even their relatives. This checkpoint was situated in Friedrichstrasse/Kochstrasse and was between the American and Soviet sectors. There had been a watchtower and fences and barriers. The site must still be a poignant reminder to the citizens of Berlin, of the division between East and West Berlin and the separation of so many families.

The Author at Gatow, helping to plant trees in memory of those who had died.

On our yearly visits to Berlin, we also have journeyed to Wunstorf, Fassburg and Lubeck. In 2000, revisiting Lubeck was very nostalgic for me, remembering my short stay there, when it had been thought I was a 'dog' (see Chapter 3). By my return visit, it was used for civil purposes (Flughaven Lubeck) and I was intrigued to find that Ryanair had a return trip to the UK for £69.

On 23rd September 1949, the last Douglas Dakota of the R.A.F. took off from Lubeck to take the last load to Gatow. The official end to the Blockade had been in May of that year but the huge operation that was the Berlin Airlift, needed time to come to a halt. We had a talk by the then director of the airfield and he was just as interested in the history of the airfield during the Airlift as we were by his description of its history and its current use. The town itself had been subject to much re-building and refurbishing of the historic buildings after the 1939/45 war ravages, followed by the period of the Airlift. I walked round the town to marvel at the buildings and I noticed the amount of lilac everywhere and the cleanliness of the town.

Lubeck was one of the Hanseatic towns. The Hanseatic League between towns of Northern Europe was created for trading purposes in the 12th century, with Lubeck taking the lead in developing trade with foreign countries. The league became very powerful, politically and commercially. However its power decreased during the 15th century with the discovery of America and the Thirty Years War, contributing to its downfall. Hamburg, Bremen and Lubeck still retain the prefix, 'Hansestadt' (Hanse-town). Lubeck is currently the biggest port in the Federal Republic of Germany. The town is situated on the Trave River which flows into Lubeck Bay, near to Travemunde, another town that we visited and enjoyed, as the hotel looked over the Bay with all of its fascinating ships.

We visited Fassburg several times. This former Royal Air Force Station played a very important part during the Airlift. There were 5399,112 tons of coal transported from this station to Berlin. I have since seen the Fassburg Flyer, an original Douglas V-47 of the US Air Force, used during the airlift and it symbolizes the co-operation between the Western Allies, the USA and the UK , plus the members of the German Civil Labour Assocation, who were responsible for loading the coal.

On one occasion, on 15th May,2004, we attended a joint commemoration service for us, with German colleagues in, 'der Michael-Kirchengemeinde (the Michael-Church).

'Okumenischer Gottesdienst anlasslich des 55 jahrigen Jubilaums der Luftbrucke Berlin'

Selig sind die bracken bauen zwishen menschen und volkern; den sie warden farben sein in Gottes regenbogen'

(Divine service on the occasion of the 5th anniversary of the end of the Berlin Airlift.

'Blessed are those who build bridges between people and nations because the will be coated with God's rainbow colours')

The service was very emotional and was meaningful to all of the congregation. Our Padre, Bill Edwards, partnered the German Pastor to lead the service. However, there moments of surprise and some jollity when we realised that the German folk were singing in German and we in English. One rendering became so difficult that the Pastor decided to play the guitar and sing the hymn as a solo. 'Herr, gib mir Mut zum Bruckenbauen, gib mir Mut zum ersten Schritt. Lass mich auf deine Bruche trauen und wenn ich gehe, geh du mit'

Roughly translated the words meant, 'Lord, give me strength to build a bridge'.

The really memorable moment came when the announcement was made that the next hymn was to be, Herbel, O ihr Glaub'gen, (O, Come, all ye Faithful), to us a very popular Christmas Carol. In the then month of May therefore, we sang it lustily, in English, whilst rest of the congregation sang equally lustily, in German. It was oddly moving, in spite of the mirth.

The last ton of coal left Fassburg on the 27th August 1949. Fassburg's flight records suggested 280,000 take-offs for the Berlin Airports Gatow, Templehof and Tegel. Many years later, in 1989, when the border reopened and the re-unification of Germany took place, Fassburg was no longer important as an operational base.

In Berlin, in 2004, we re-visited the German Bundestag Building (Parliament). When visiting the Reichstag in previous years, I had not been able to go up to the Dome, as it entails travelling in a lift, not my favourite occupation. I had heard from my colleagues that the Reichstag was built from 1884 until 1894 in the style of the Italian High Renaissance and it served as the seat of Parliament in the Kaiserrich and Weimar Republic.

The Reichstag fire in 1933 (which I vaguely remember but had no understanding at the time, being only six years old), completely destroyed the plenary chamber. It was also heavily damaged in the 1939/45 war and total reconstruction lasted until 1970. Since 1994 the edifice has been rebuilt and renovated according to the plans of Norman Foster.

In 1999, the Reichstag was reopened and now serves as the seat of the Federal Government – the Bunderstag. The huge and magnificent Dome is open to the public and it is composed of two double helixes, which means that it is possible to walk all over the Dome's surface, walking up paths that seem to cling to the curved surface. Feeling sorry that I was not able to see this marvel for myself, I went outside and met Heinz-Gerde Rees, a great friend of the Association. He suddenly disappeared and came back with two girls, one very tall, thin and the obvious leader, called Badre and a small pretty girl named Katerin.

They had minor roles in the Reichstag staff and had been persuaded to find a way up to the Dome for me. They spoke no English and my German was, and is, miniscule. We climbed stairs, ran along obviously 'private' corridors, went through rooms that needed security passes and up more stairs with the word 'Verboten' in, large print. Badre shut her eyes every time a notice appeared! I was being dragged along, having no idea where we were and in no position to object. We came to a bell tower with a very narrow staircase and we ran up to find a guard, in a cubby hole, sitting at a desk. He looked astonished. Badre gesticulated to him that we were just passing through and he was still staring blankly at us as we passed through a door into the Dome.

The view of the Berlin was breathtaking and I also had the experience of negotiating the double helixes that formed the shape of the whole structure and then magically negotiating these curves, by walking round the Dome. Then of course I had to return to the ground floor. The guard just looked bemused as we ran past him and hurtled down the stairs and back down the corridors and even more stairs, until I reached the pavement and the safety of our coach. Nevertheless, I had seen the Reichstag, the Dome and impressively the huge room where the German Parliament meet.

I was fascinated by the historic avenue, Unter den Linden, (Beneath the Lime Trees) which leads from the past centre of Berlin, in the east, which leads up to the Brandenburger Tor. There is a mile of famous shops, royal palaces, museums and by various consulate buildings. This famous avenue crosses the campus of the Humboldt University and also by the great shopping centre of the Friedrichstrasse. The Brandenburg Tor (Gate) is the only remaining city gate and is still of great importance to the city as it became the symbol of the separation of East and West. The Gate was re-opened in December 1989, after the destruction of the Wall.

With mixed feelings, I remember the visit to the Mohne Dam. The bombing of this dam in 1943, was the subject of the film, 'The Dam Busters' and therefore, to me, had an aura of romanticism, which swiftly evaporated when my visit led me to understand the immensity of the whole operation. It is now a magnificent structure, having been rebuilt. The Mohnsee Lake is very beautiful, placed in countryside surrounded by trees and grass and it was obvious why the aircraft had to fly at low altitudes. Apparently the bouncing bomb, invented by Barnes Wallis, had to hit the bottom of the dam, following which, it took two days to properly disintegrate the dam structure. The village at the end of the lake, was destroyed and has also been rebuilt.

We sensed a bitterness, even then (2001), by the local people, in contrast to the majority of German civilians whom we met in all our relationships in the Airlift, who seemed everlastingly grateful to us for supporting them during the Blockade. From the film, I had envisaged the lake surrounded by an industrial area, protected by large numbers of troops. In reality, the reason for the destruction of the dam was because of its production of energy for a very wide area, thus it was mainly civilians who were the casualties. I read later that Barnes Wallis himself realised the awful consequences of the bouncing bomb, even though it was pronounced a triumph. He continued with his work however and later helped with the design of the Concorde Civil aircraft, was knighted in 1968 and died in 1979.

We visited Hannover several times, particularly interesting to me, as I had had several sorties there whilst I was stationed at Bad Eilsen. I was aware that in 1714, George Ludvig of Hannover became George 1st of England. The Stuart King, James 1st arranged for two of his children to marry continental rulers, Charles 1st, who married Henrietta, daughter of the French King. Their descendants later ruled England, as Charles 2nd, James 2 nd, William 3rd and Queen Anne. Elizabeth Stuart however, married the Elector Frederick of the Palantine (Heidelberg) and her daughter Sophie married the future Elector of Hannover, Duke Ernst August. As the British parliament had decreed a Protestant successor only to the throne, the great grandson of James 1st, through this female succession became not only the king of Scotland but of England too. In fact the association between England and Hannover lasted through until the beginning of Victoria's reign in 1937.

During the 1939/45 war Hannover was all but destroyed and only a few of its old buildings remained. When I visited there in 1948/9, the town, the capital of the Federal land of Lower Saxony was having a re-birth. I remember rubble and piles of bricks and stones. When I visited in 2001, the town was beautiful. Our hotel was opposite to the Rathaus (Town Hall), where there was an exhibition of models of the town, which showed the different 'Hannovers' over the centuries, especially before and after the Second World War.

Over the years, we have been invited to the theatre and to wonderful meals by the Mayor of Berlin, we were invited to visit the British Embassy, to museums, particularly those in Berlin, Fassburg and Wunstorf, and enjoyed trips on the river. We have attended memorial ceremonies in places where an event of note had taken place, laying wreaths and with the inclusion of a service, usually led by our padre. I have diaries of every trip that I have made with the British Berlin Airlift Association and perhaps therein lies a future book.

Worthy of recording now, is the Association's memorable ceremony on Sunday 29th June,2008, to celebrate the 60th anniversary of the Airlift. We had a splendid day in Peterborough, where we marched though the town, accompanied by the RAF Wyton Voluntary Band. We veterans were led by bearers, carrying the BBAA Standard, the Standard of the British Legion and the Standards of many other Associations. There were representatives from the United States Air Force, from USAF Alconbury, led by Colonel Jordan , members of the No. 85 Expeditionary Logistics Wings from RAF Wittering and delegates from three local Air Training Corps Squadrons. The Mayor of Peterborough, Cllr Mrs Patricia A.Nash MBE, took the salute in front of the Town Hall accompanied by Wing Commander Andrew Curtis from RAF Wittering and Colonel Jordan from USAF Alconbury. The parade finished at the parish church of St. John, where the commemoration service was conducted by Canon Gordon Steele and our Padre, Rev. William (Bill) Edwards, with BBAA members, Group Captain Colin Parry and William (Bill) Campbell, reading the lessons, which was a fitting part of our day's celebrations.

Another highlight to mark the 60th anniversary of the completion of the Berlin Airlift was the splendid service of commemoration that took place on Saturday 26th September 2009, at the National Memorial Nr. Lichfeld, Staffordshire and was established in 1997 and after being conceived as a living tribute to all those who have died in service to their country. There are 150 acres of trees and permanent memorial walls, upon which are recorded the names of those who had laid down their lives.

At this 60th anniversary of the Airlift, there were 530 veterans , friends and families and also serving personnel for this celebration, which marked the final flight of the Airlift. Among the distinguished guests were Minister Kevan Jones and the new Chief of the Air Staff, Air Chief Marshal, Sir Stephen Dalton, themselves veterans and many senior representatives from France, Germany and America.

I remember it as a joyous day, with a service conducted by our own padre, Bill Edwards MA, along with the Venerable Ray J.Pentland QHC BA Mth RAF, Archdeacon for the Royal air Force, with readings given by representatives of the British Berlin Airlift Association. A highlight was a message of thanks on behalf of the people of Berlin, from their Mayor, Klaus Wowereit, read out by Brigadier General Franz-Josef Nolte, the Defence and Air Attache from the German Embassy in London. We of course, remembered the 39 British and Commonwealth personnel, who died during the Airlift. Their names are remembered permanently at the Arboretum.

We had music from the RAF Regiment Band and the Black Watch Voluntary Band and the commemoration had a tremendous finish with the Royal Air Force Aerobatic team, the Red Arrows, who flew over the Arboretum. The whole day summed up for me our feeling of pride at the achievement during 1948/9, when so many servicemen and women and the vast number of civilians involved, kept the people of Berlin and indeed Berlin itself, alive during the Soviet Blockade.

The programme, setting out the order of the day was lucky enough to include a Foreword by Prince Charles, Duke of Cornwall.

Herewith his message:

'The Berlin Airlift was one of the most remarkable feats in history. The role played by our Armed Forces in keeping the population of Berlin alive during 1948-1949 – precisely at the time that I was born – was by all accounts incredibly difficult, dangerous and at some times, seemingly impossible.

In this 60th anniversary year, we remember all those who took part but particularly the thirty nine British personnel and civilian and ground crew who lost their loves in ensuring others survived.

During my visit to Berlin earlier this year, I was shown round the Allied Museum by Larry Lamb, the Vice President of the British Berlin Airlift Association. It was particularly fascinating to learn more about the Airlift, - the conditions our Armed Forces operated in, for instance and the selfless dedication of our servicemen and women who helped the people of Berlin, so soon after the Second World War.

I know that the servicemen and women of our Armed Forces today are called upon to display the same courage, discipline, selfless commitment, integrity, loyalty and respect for others as their forbears did sixty years ago. We owe all British Berlin Airlift Veterans, civilians and their families of those who lost their lives, a vast debt of gratitude.'

(Signed 'Charles')

In 2012 and 2014, I received letters from Gunther Herzog, from his home in Buckeburg. He is a member of the British Association, the Bad Eilsen Reunion, to which all those who have ever served in Bad Eilsen were invited to join in order to keep in touch with each other. The members had kindly contacted me with reference to Gunther, as they knew that he had served at Bad Eilsen during the Airlift, in a civilian capacity. I contacted Gunther and in his informative reply, which included photographs, it seemed highly likely that we had worked in the same building at times, with our jobs being similar. It is sad, now looking back to the past, that we were not encouraged to talk to those civilians with whom we worked, in at least a more social way. He knew the house in which I was billeted and also visited Scharfoldendorf to learn to glide, though, seemingly at different times than the RAF personnel. Even more coincidental, he visited Neuhaus, to join in one of the groups of German Youth and RAF personnel of much the same age group, as I did of course. He was not there at the same time as I but he remembers the officers concerned. He was also invited to act as interpreter.

Gunther said that, after the war, he originally volunteered for farming but the farmer could not accommodate him in the winter months, so he returned home and both he and his sister Helga, worked in the Kurmittel House, in Bad Eilsen. He did return to school for six months as the 'Nazi tests', taken in his earlier teens were invalid. He started as a 'runner' in the Bade Hotel and also printed out the Unit Routine Orders, which he also dispatched. He told me that Flt. Lt. Robin Wade had given him some 'parallel pliers', which he still uses to this day. The Civil Labour Office gave him a job on Buckeburg Airfield, digging cables for the flare paths. He said, 'We were ordered to leave the digging when the 'Meteors' flew over. One of the boys wanted to stay where he was, resulting in a pilot flying right over him. He did not do it again.'

Gunther wrote in English, which I admired, never having acquired a useful knowledge of German myself. However, sometimes there was a lack of coherence, so making some difficulties for me in extracting his actual intended meaning. He did write, rather sadly, 'I often heard Brits say that all Germans were Nazis. This is very different over Germany'. He explained that Munchen, at the time of the war, was the town of the movement and Nuremburg was the town of the 'Party'. He suggested also that Bad Eilsen as a Spa had, 'parties there that were a mixture of groups with nationalistic tendencies'. He added that Bremen was a ship building community and largely communistic.

Gunther's Father was obliged by his boss, to join at least one Nazi group and he reluctantly joined the Reich-Colonial

Federation, which he was sure was not really Nazi. He advised Gunther to research an exhibition in the market, which was about the Freemasons. He apparently learned through this exhibition that this group was indeed not Nazi and within the anti-aircraft troop, their commanders were all Freemasons.

Gunther himself had been forced to fire guns at aircraft during the war – he must have been very young and hardly aware of the danger he was in, or why it was necessary for him to effect these manoeuvres.

His life altered when he was able to return home, go back to school for six months and work on the Airlift at Bad Eilsen, where he was also involved in a Drama group, which gave him much pleasure.

I have written at some length about Gunther, as we have not always been aware of how the Germans themselves felt about the war or indeed how the Airlift impacted on their lives, especially living outside of Berlin. I remember Ingrid, Gunther and Herr Seufert and how the war impinged upon their lives, with their insecurity continuing afterwards, with the unrest of the Cold War, which even now remains, under a very thin surface of temporary truce.

In 1998, my sister Audrey and brother-in-law Harold, paid a visit to Newark Air Museum (Notts. and Lincs.), where there was a collection of British, American and European Aircraft. Several ex-RAF servicemen were there as 'guides' and during the interesting tour, I mentioned to the men accompanying us, that I had been in the WAAF and that I had served on the Berlin Airlift. The men firstly looked surprised, then rather excited. They informed us that I was the first 'lady' Airlifter that they had ever met, which tickled us immensely, particularly as one or two of them had served on the Airlift. Their comment did confirm the age-old concept that women are not often considered adequate for manly pursuits. Even today! Certainly in 1948, there were no women pilots flying goods to Gatow but despite male prejudices, many high ranking and important jobs were successfully effected by women.

The next surprise was in being shown a Hastings aircraft that had actually flown on the Airlift. We were even taken inside and I immediately remembered the air sickness I suffered when flying to Lubeck. The inside of the Hastings, with the internal structure on show, the inadequate seating and the feeling of a lack of stability, even though it was on the ground, brought back all the miseries of my Lubeck journey. I was thrilled to see the 'plane however and was delighted when I was invited to join the men who had looked after us for the afternoon in a photograph, especially as it was taken by the side of the aircraft.

The memory of the Airlift, of how we worked together the effort, the loyalty and the commitment, will always be with me. Maybe the whole operation did not achieve the peace for Germany, indeed Europe, that was so desired. The past thousands of years had proved that there will always be the power seekers, those who want to dominate others and those who want to acquire land and territories, whatever the cost.

However, within the remit of that one year, which was to support the besieged people of Berlin, to keep them fed and heated and able them to function in such a way that it was possible to revive the city after the cessation of the Blockade, we can say, that we did achieve the miracle. Too many people died, from many nationalities. There were 39 British men who died. We will remember them.

Last Thoughts

No More
No more to see the airfields, scattered around the land
No more to see the airmen, with their irons in their hand
No more to see the ensign raised, standing smartly to attention
No more to hear the S.W.O shout, things we dare not mention
No more to see the airman, as the stones he paints
No more in that mess to hear, 'Orderly Office, any complaints'
No more to hear the Royal Air Force march, as the station paraded
No more to march to music that through the years has faded
No more to hear the engines, doing their morning ground run
No more to see the props rotating, like halos in the sun
No more to feel the powerful lift, beneath the aircraft's win
No more the roar of engines, as their pistons in unison sing
No more to see your squadron, in formation in the air
No more to see your aircraft type, for they are no longer there
No more to see the Ensign Lowered, as the sun sets in the West
No more to see the airmen that through the years have stood the test

Poem written by William (Bill) Ball, who took part in the Airlift at Wunstorf and Lubeck ,in the Flight Line, in the 77 Squadron. He was present when the very first 'plane took off from Wunstorf, taking supplies to Gatow, June 1948.

Bibliography

The sources of my material were mainly from my own diaries and memorabilia.
Letters and information kindly sent to me, were mentioned in the text, as they were used.

From the valuable notes and knowledge afforded me over the years, particularly in the lectures on Europe, I am grateful to my history Tutor, *Ann Lewis Jones.*

British Berlin Airlift Association Newsletters , in particular, issues December 2006, December 2007, December 2008, Summer 2009 and December 2013, gave valuable recollections and information from the members.

There were several instances of permission sought for use of material, which remained unanswered. I therefore thank all the sources used and have kept the integrity of the information as far as possible.

Books

Gere Edwin, *The Unheralded*, 2002, Trafford Publishing

Huschke Wolfgang. J., *The Candy Bombers, A History of people and 'Planes*, 1999, Printed by H&H.Russ GmbH, Berlin

Man John, *The Leadership Secrets Of Ghengis Khan*, 2009, pub. Bantam Press (Transworld Pub.)

Taylor, Frederick, *The Berlin Wall*, 2007, Bloomsbury Publishing Plc.

Tusa, John @ Ann (1998), *The Berlin Airlift*, pub. Spellmount

Note: Many photographs and pictures, mentioned in the text were old and of poor quality.
 The decision was therefore reluctantly made, that they unsuitable for use in the book.

Appendix 1- Diary of Events – 1948 to 1949

June 1948

17th - A plan was prepared by HQ BAFO for the supply of British servicemen by air – coded 'Knicker'
24th - All land and water communications to and from Berlin were stopped by the Soviets.
25th - RAF Dakotas of Transport Command flew from the UK to Wunstorf
28th - The first Dakotas took off from Wunstorf to Gatow. HQ Army Air Transport Organisation & a Rear Airfield Supply Org. formed at Wunstorf.
29th - 21st birthday of ACW.1 Peachey. J.L. (Now Joyce Hargrave-Wright)
30th - The whole operation was then named 'Carter Paterson'

July 1948

1st - York Aircraft sent from the UK to Wunstorf
3rd - Yorks began operating on the Airlift
5th - Sunderland flying boats began operating from Finkenwerder(the Elbe) to Lake Havel, Berlin
7th -Big day! The first coal was flown into Berlin by Dakotas
10th -HQ Army Air Transport moved to the Schloss, Buckeburg.
16th -The concrete runways at Gatow were finished and ready for flights.
19th -The Name of the British Airlift operation was finally named 'Operation Plainfare'
20th -2,250 tons of supplies were sent to Berlin in 24 hours by both the RAF and the USAF
27th The first civil aircraft, a Lancastrian used on the Airlift flew from Buckeburg to Berlin

29th -The RAF Dakotas based at Wunstorf & twin-engined civil aircraft transferred to Fassberg.

August 1948

4th -First day of formal Civil Airlift. Charter 'planes based at Finkenwerder,Fassburg&Wunstorf
20th -RAF Dakotas transferred from Fassburg to Lubeck
 Dakotas worked simultaneously from both stations whilst the changeover took place
21st -USAF C-54 aircraft moved into Fassburg and operated into Gatow.

September 1948

14th -The Deputy Chief of Air Staff and the AOC-in Charge Transport Command, with the AOC No. 46 Group visited A.H.Q BAFO to discuss matters of the Airlift with the AOC in Control BAFO.
15th -Arrival of RAAF Squadrons of 12 aircrews at Lubeck. Construction of runway at RAF Celle started.
18th -Instructions issued for attachment of an advanced operational element of H.Q. No. 46 Group to BAFO under the command of Air Commodore J.W.F. Merer, A.O.C 46 Group.
20th -The advance party of three officers and one airmen of the operational H.Q. arrived from the UK and occupied offices in the Schloss, Buckeburg.
22nd -The A.O.C No. 46 Group, ten officers and seven airmen arrived at Buckeburg from UK to form No.46 group Advanced Operational H.Q.

30th -At a conference held at A.H.Q. BAFO, the A.O.C. agreed in principle to a combined USAF/RAF Headquarters for the Airlift

October 1948

5th -Civil-twin engine aircraft based at Lubeck moved to Fuhlsbuttel(Hamburg)

7th -Notification by HQ Transport command of decision to operate Hastings aircraft on the Airlift. A total of 442 short tons was flown into Gatow by British Aircraft in 24 hours, the highest to date.

8th - Decision to open Schleswigland as a Plainfare base to accommodate Hastings aircraft

13th - Major General Tunner, USAF, the Commander-designate of the Combined Airlift Task Force visited HQ No. 46 Group to discuss details of its organisation.

15th - Establishment of H.Q. Combined Airlift Task Force announced, in a combined directive issued by A.O.C.-in-C , B.A.F.O and the Commanding General U.S.F.A.E. Major General Tunner was appointed Commander, C.A.L.T.F and Air Commodore Merer was appointed Deputy Commander. A South African Air Force Squadron arrived at Lubeck to take part in Operation Plainfare. Conference at H.Q. No. 46 Group to decide methods of utilisation of British Civil aircraft and crews on the airlift.

17th - 454 short tons flown into Gatow in a 24-hour period by British aircraft

19th - The backloading of German civilians from Berlin to Lubeck by RAF Dakotas began.

21st - The A.O.C. and the Staff Officers of No. 46 group attended a conference at HQ. C.A.L.T.F to discuss the detailed c-ordination of the British and American effort.

16th - Arrival Of R.N.Z.A.F. aircrews at Lubeck

November 1948

1st - First Squadron of Hastings arrived at Schleswigland to join the Airlift Standard Operation procedures, in amplification of Transport Command Air Staff Instructions, issued by H.Q. No. 46 Group

3rd - The 300,000th short ton flown into Berlin by British and American aircraft

8th - The Secretary of State for Air arrived from the U.K. for a tour of Airlift Stations

11th - First Hastings aircraft operated on the Airlift

18th - First Dakota from Lubeck landed at Tegel, the new airfield in the French sector of Berlin

22nd - The 500,000 short ton flown into Berlin by British and American aircraft

25th - British Civil 4–engined aircraft began operations from Schleswigland

December 1948

1st -Transfer of administrative control of RAF Plainfare Stations from BAFO to No. 46 Group. Tegel (Berlin) airfield formally opened for traffic.

8th - H.Q.B.A.F.O. issued a directive to A.O.C. No. 46 group defining the operational and Administrative aspects of Operation Plainfare

15th - U.S.A.F. C-54 aircraft moved into Celle

16th - Sunderland flying boats withdrawn from the Airlift. Finkenwerder closed. First Airlift sortie flown by the U.S.A.F c-54s based at Celle

25th - The 50,000th landing by an aircraft at Gatow was made by a Dakota from Lubeck

28th - This day marked the first six months of Operation Plainfare. The American Airlift commenced on 26th June,1948. The combined

total tonnage, (RAF, Civil and USAF) flown into Berlin during this period was 700,172 short tons in 96,640 sorties
31st - The 100,000 sortie into Berlin by British,Civil and USAF aircraft

January 1949

1st - Highest weekly total to date of 41,287 short tons flown by the Combined Airlift
15th - Tegel received the first British Civil aircraft.
19th - Three quarter millionth short ton by the Combined Airlift was delivered to Berlin
20th - The Chief of the Air Staff arrived in Germany on a visit to Airlift Stations.
26th - Conference at H.Q. Bo 46 Group to discuss contracts for Civil Charter Companies and to recommend amendments in the light of experience to date.
31st -Highest monthly total to date lifted by the Combined Airlift – 171,960 short tons.

February 1949

1st - Meteorological Forecasting Section established at H.Q. No. 46 group
3rd - Highest tonnage to date in 24 hours lifted by British aircraft – 1,736 tons in 203 sorties.
15th - Air Ministry decision promulgated that flying boats would not be re-employed on the
Airlift in the following Spring.
16th - Air Ministry Conference to consider the policy for the relief of aircrews employed on the Airlift.
18th - The millionth ton by the C.A.L.T.F. was flown into Berlin in an RAF York from Wunstorf. The airlift had lasted 7 months and 24 days.

March 1949

4th - The Prime Minister arrived at Buckeburg to inspect Airlift stations.
11th - The RAF flew to Lubeck the 50,000th German civilian brought out of Berlin
15th - H.Q. No. 46 group moved from Buckeburg to Luneburg
31st - Highest monthly tonnage to date lifted by the C.A.L.T.F. – 196, 160 short tons

April 1949

1st - Transfer of H.Q. No. 46 Group from Transport Command to BAFO. Civil Airlift Division (BEA) formed in Berlin
11th - Highest tonnage to date in 24 hours lifted by C.A.L.T.F. 8246 short tons in 922 sorties. RAF and British Civil aircraft at Wunstorf contributed 1,135 short tons, the highest total to date from that station.
12th -Dakotas from Lubeck commenced to lift 1st Batt. Royal Welsh Fusiliers to relieve 1st Batt., Norfolk Regiment.
16th - in a special effort to test the Airlift organisation, C.A.L.T.F. carried 12,940 short tons in 1,398 sorties, of which 2035 short tons were British carried 2035.
17th - Highest British daily lift to date – 2086 short tons
30th - Highest monthly tonnage to date lifted by C.A.L.T.F – 232, short tons

May 1949

1st -Civil Airlift division (BEA) joined H.Q. No. 46 Group at Luneburg
5th -Agreement reached between the Western Powers and Russia that the blockade would be lifted on 12th May.
9th - Highest British tonnage in 24-hour period flown into Berlin – 2,167 short tons.

12th - The Berlin Blockade was lifted at 0001 hours. Highest British tonnage in 24 hour period – 2,183 short tons Dakotas from Lubeck commenced to lift the 1st Batt. Gordon Highlanders to Berlin to relieve the 1st Battt. Worcs. Regiment.

From thence it took several months to wind-down the whole project, to return the Servicemen/women home, to transfer the aircraft to their 'home' stations and for the Berliners to start to return to some sort of normality.

This timetable did not exhibit any knowledge of its author or of the history of its possible extraction from an article or journal. I have tried to establish the ownership with no success. I acknowledge my thanks to the author in his/her absence.

Appendix 2 - Aircraft Facts and Figures

Tonnage lifted to Berlin by British Aircraft
RAF Aircraft 249509 tons
Civil Aircraft 147727 tons
Total 542236 tons

Tonnage lifted to Berlin by USAF aircraft
1783572.7 tons

Total combined British and American Airlift tonnage
2325808.7 tons

Tonnage by Type
Food
(British)241712.9 tons
(USAF) 296303.1 tons
Coal (British) 164799.7 tons
(USAF) 1421729.6 tons
Military (British)18239.1 tons
Liquid Fuel (British) 92282.4 tons
Miscellaneous (British)25201.1 tons}

Military (USAF) 65540 tons

British Tonnage Exported from Berlin
  35843.1 tons

Passengers lifted to and from Berlin

British **To** 36218 **From** 131436
American **To** 24216 **From** 36584

Total **To** 60434 **From** 168020

Highest Daily Combined British and American Tonnage
12940.9 tons on 16th April, 1949

Highest Daily British Tonnage
2314.5 on 5th July 1949

Highest Daily RAF Tonnage
1735.6 tons on 17th August 1948

Highest Daily British Civil Tonnage
1.bought 9.61009.6 tons on 22th May 1949

British aircraft consumed over 35,000,000 gallons of aviation fuel, flew more than 30,000,000 miles, and spent more than 200,000 hours in the air, flying to and from Berlin.

(From, 'Britain and the Berlin Airlift', RAF Air Historical Branch booklet (no date given)

Appendix 3: Names of those who lost their lives

This list records the names of the 39 British and Commonwealth men, who lost their lives in the air and on the ground, whilst taking part in the Berlin Airlift Operation, from June 28th, 1948 until September 30th 1949 and thus ensured the survival of the city.

Anderson, John   30th April,1949
Burton, Alan John   22nd November, 1948
Carroll, Edward Ernest   30th April,1949
Casey, Michael Edwin   22nd November, 1948
Cusack, William   22nd November, 1948
Donaldson, Ian Ronald   16th July, 1949
Dowling, Frank   17th November, 1948
Dunsire, Alexander   16th July, 1949
Edwards, Peter James   15th March, 1949
Freight, Robert John   21st March, 1949
Gibbs, Roy Reginald   16th July, 1949
Gilbert, Lawrence Edward Hope   19th September,1948
Golding, Cecil   15th March, 1949
Griffin, Patrick James   15th January, 1949
Grout, John Ernest   24th January. 1949
Heath, Reginald Merrick Watson   22nd November, 1948
Kell, Geoffrey   19th September, 1948
Lewis, William Richard Donald   30th April, 1049
Louch, Philip Arthur   17th November, 1948
Newman, Henry Thomas   15th March, 1949
O'Neil, Edward   15th January, 1949
Page, William George   16th July, 1949
Patterson, Henry   21st March, 1949
Penny, Alan (AFC)   22nd March. 1949
Quinn, Mel Joseph   22nd March, 1949
Reeves, Kenneth Arthur   22nd March, 1949

Robertson, Dornford Winston 22nd March, 1949
Seabourne, Kenneth Arthur 22nd November, 1948
Sharp, James Patrick Lewin 21st March, 1949
Supernatt, Theodor 15th January, 1949
Taylor, Cyril DFC FM 22nd November, 1948
Thomson, Hugh Wallace MC DFC 19th September, 1948
Toal, Joseph 16th July, 1949
Towersey, Sidney Mark Lewis 19th September. 1948
Trezona, Francis Ivor 17th November, 1948
Utting, Clement Wilbur 8th December, 1948
Watson, Ernest William 19th September, 1948
Wilkins, John Graham 25th November, 1948
Wood, Kenneth George 30th April, 1949

Information taken from 'The Berlin Airlift', the programme and Order of Service, for the 'Service of Thanksgiving and Commemoration of the 60th Anniversary of the end of the Berlin Airlift', which took place at the National Memorial Arboretum, Alrewas, Staffordshire on Saturday 26th September, 2009.